A Yoder Branch
From
Swiss Roots

The Ancestors and Descendants of Reuben K. Yoder

By
Ronald F. Yoder

Published by the Author
In
The United States of America

Printed by
CreateSpace

Additional copies can be obtained at:
www.createspace.com/4423774

ISBN-13: 978-1492296423

ISBN-10: 1492296422

Dedication

I would like to lovingly dedicate this book to my grandchildren. I am proud that they will carry forward the Yoder name for our branch.

Addison J Yoder

Greer E Yoder

Graydon E Yoder

Bryce G Yoder

Zane D Yoder

Genealogy

Is much like treasure hunting

Except that,

In genealogy,

Many more gems are found.

Contents

Preface

This work is considered private and is primarily intended for use by the descendants of Reuben K. and Mary M. Yoder. It is my effort of more than thirty years to collect data on the ancestors and descendants of Reuben and Mary. The branches continue to grow so the work will never be complete, but it is intended to provide some insight into where the Yoders came from, or more specifically where *our* Yoders came from, should some future generation be so inquisitive.

While I have attempted to make the data as accurate as possible, perfection is not guaranteed and you may find mistakes. Misspellings and transpositions have a way of being overlooked even with careful editing and multiple checks. I have tried to cite all reference material; unfortunately, some may have been overlooked.

At several places I have referenced our European ancestors. I want to emphasize that these links, while they may be correct, as of this writing are *unverified*.

And finally, I want to give due credit to the *Yoder Newsletter* and to the book *Amish and Amish Mennonite Genealogies*. I have used direct quotes from these sources and relied heavily on them as my main references. To anybody interested, I would recommend purchasing these items.

Subscriptions for YNL can be ordered from: *Yoder Newsletter*, PO Box 594, Goshen, IN 46527-0595

Amish and Amish Mennonite Genealogies can be ordered from; Masthof Press, 219 Mill Road, Morgantown, PA 19543-9516

I hope you enjoy reading about our ancestors as much as I have enjoyed researching and writing about them.

Ronald F. Yoder
Thompsontown, PA

Forward

In the 30ᵗʰ anniversary issue of the *Yoder Newsletter*, while discussing the beginnings of that paper, the editor Chris Yoder noted "we were able to stand on the shoulders of many great historians". I would like to borrow his statement because I, too, feel the same way about the contents of this book.

The product contained in this book was the result of much work and many, many hours of research by myself and others, both in the US and in Europe. I have gathered the results of the previous researcher's labor for use by our own families.

I would have probably given up my quest were it not for Chris Yoder and the *Yoder Newsletter*. Chris has helped me directly and indirectly and many times my quest for information has led me back to the *Yoder Newsletter*'s archive of data. At times this became frustrating, pursuing what I thought was a brilliant idea only to find that YNL had already researched the same data.

My next source of information was the book *Amish and Amish Mennonite Genealogies* by Hugh F. Gingerich and Rachel W. Kreider. These two people and their book absolutely amaze me. They researched all of the original Amish immigrant surnames (there were more than 140 of them), and then traced their descendants through more than 100 years into the mid and late 1800's. If a person is of Amish descent and they know their great-grandfather's name, chances are he is in this book and it will lead them back to their original immigrant.

Another great research tool is the book *Only A Twig* by Lois Ann Zook. While this book was written to trace the lineage of the Zooks, it also contains information about many other Amish families including our own Grandmother Mary Zook. This book also brings the ancestors closer to today.

Unknowingly, this book was to be the impetus and model for my work.

At a recent Yoder reunion, Cousin Dennis King used the book, *Only A Twig* to tell the gathering about our grandmother Mary Mae (Zook) Yoder. Sometime following that reunion, Dennis mentioned that it would be nice to have a book similar to *Only A Twig* for our Yoder branch.

For some time, I had been hoping that one of the younger people in our family would take an interest in genealogy and I would be able to pass my findings on to him/her. That did not seem to be happening, so one day while thinking about this I remembered Dennis' musings and wondered why I couldn't put into book form the information that I had collected. What follows is my attempt to do that.

Additionally, Dennis agreed to collect any of the memories our cousins may have about Reuben and Mary and of their own parents (Eighth generation) and include them in this book.

I have mentioned several of my research materials, and while they were my main sources, they are by far not the only ones. Many people have helped me and provided me with information, including my sister Donna and my first cousins. Many thanks to them for sharing the latest information about their families and for their contribution of memories.

I especially want to thank my wife Gloria and Cousin Dennis. Gloria for her uncomplaining and tireless efforts reading and editing this work over and over again and making it infinitely more readable, and Dennis for volunteering to collect the "Memories" and putting them together for this book. I also want to thank my grandson Addison for helping me with some difficult formatting issues. My heartfelt thanks to them and to all who contributed.

Chapter 1
The Yoder Name

To explain the origin of the Yoder name, I have copied the following data from <u>Wikipedia</u> and from the <u>Yoder Newsletter</u> (published in Goshen, IN by Editor Chris Yoder)

From The Yoder Newsletter

All American Yoders whose ancestry is known or suspected, trace their lineage to the Joder clan in the canton of Bern in Switzerland. They are a very old family, apparently of Germanic-Swiss stock, yet the name comes from St. Theodore (Theodorus, Theodulus) a missionary monk who, in the fourth century, crossed the Alps from Italy to bring the Gospel to the Valais country in southern Switzerland. This patron saint was held in ever greater reverence as time went on.

One of Several Joder Crests

Joder Huebel (Yoder Hill) is a natural fortress on the Emme River in the southern part of the canton of Bern. Since it was so named as far back as anyone can remember and Joders were said to have lived there in the middle ages, researcher Karl Joder of Ludwigshafen-am-Rhein (West Germany) believes the family must have lived there before recorded history. The oldest record he has found is of a Peter Joder born in Joder Huebel in 1260. In 1389 a grandson Ulli Joder and his son Heini were among the heaviest taxpayers at Huttwil, a town about thirty miles north. Karl Joder is confident that the Joders found later in nearby towns can be traced back to Ulli ... including those of the town of Steffisburg.

Steffisburg, located near Thun south of Bern, is truly the home place of many American Yoders and in discussing our European origins we shall refer to Steffisburg again and again. Here Joders lived for generations as farmers, brewers, millers and other varying occupations. They were active in the affairs of both church and state and a number of heraldic banners (coats-of-arms) are set in stained glass at the old Steffisburg church, which was the center of a large parish. The town was not only a center for the State Church (Swiss Reformed), but for the Anabaptist sympathizers as well, who believed in the separation of church and state.

As in many instances where people must choose between differing ideas, the Joder family had members on both sides of the religious fence. Many were quite prominent participants in Reformed Church activities, and others were attracted to the Anabaptists.

From Steffisburg, Joders of both groups migrated north at the end of the 17th century and early decades of the 18th. They settled in Neustadt, Annweilerhof, Oggersheim, Mussbach, and Eppstein in the Palatinate of west central Germany. The Anabaptists (known as Swiss Brethren and later Mennonites ... and the followers of Jacob Amman from nearby Erlenbach who came to be called "Amish") fled at the turn of the century for refuge in not only the Palatinate, but Alsace-Lorraine as well. Many of the Anabaptist group in particular eventually moved on to America.

Elsewhere, some of these immigrants to the New World are discussed. Although they and their descendants will quite naturally receive the lion's share of attention, the Joder family has certainly not vanished from the "Old World" countries of today. A 1940 list of Mennonite family names of South Germany showed 34 Jothers among six separate congregations. Seven people named Yoder, Ioder, or Jother were members of

French Mennonite churches as of 1951. Descendants of one Steffisburg Joder family are reported to have moved to Rumania and Eastern Europe where they are said to be living still.

In spite of considerable migration, many Joders remain in the ancestral homeland. In a visit to Switzerland in 1980 it was found that five Joders appeared in the Steffisburg phone directory and six Joders were identified in the phonebook of the capital city of Bern.

From Wikipedia

The name Yoder is first found in the region of Westphalia, in the old Saxon territory, which is found in the modern-day region of Bundesland. Westphalia was part of the old duchy of Saxony. The surname is a shortened version of Theodorus, the name of the first Roman Catholic bishop of Sion (bishop of Octodurum) in present day Martigny, Switzerland. Theodorus—also known as St. Theodore of Grammont, St. Theodule, and St. Joder—is the patron saint of Triesenberg, Liechtenstein.

The surname Yoder is derived from the name Theodorus. Distinguished University of Notre Dame theologian John Howard Yoder has explained step-by-step how the evolution from Theodorus to Yoder was the result of simple, normal changes in pronunciation. The surname Yoder probably developed from the name Theodorus by taking the following turns:

Sanctus Theodorus
Sanctus Tjordorus
Sankt Tjoder
Sant Tjoder
Sant Joder
(Saint) Yoder

3

The name Joder is most common in Switzerland and is widespread there. In the United States, the leap from "Joder" to "Yoder" was natural because the English spelling of the latter name phonetically reflects the German pronunciation of the name.

Alternate spellings of the surname include:

Joder	Jotter	Jordi	Ioder
Jodier	Yother	Yodis	Yothers
Yordi	Yotter	Yordy	

Saint Theodorus

Theodorus was a 4th century missionary-monk who crossed the Alps from Italy to establish a Catholic outpost in the Valais region of southern Switzerland.

Legend

According to a well-circulated legend, in 350 AD while in Agaunum, Theodorus found the bones of Saint Maurice and the legendary Theban legion. Theodorus is said to have then built a basilica on the land where the bones were found. Around the year 515, the site was later converted to a monastery after the surrounding land was donated by Sigismund. The monastery is now known as Abbey of Saint-Maurice d'Agaune.

According to hagiographical material, the Theban legion was entirely composed of Christians. They had been called from Thebes in Egypt to assist Maximian in Gaul in modern day France. However, when Maximian ordered the legion to sacrifice to the Emperor and to suppress Christianity in Gaul, they refused. Subsequently, Maximian ordered the unit punished. Every tenth soldier was killed, a military punishment known as decimation. More orders followed, but the legion still refused to comply, and a second decimation was

4

ordered. Because after the second decimation the legion still refused to use violence against fellow Christians, Maximian ordered all the remaining members of the unit executed.

Some historians suggest that the story of Maurice and the Theban legion was a pious fabrication created by either Theodorus or Eucherius, bishop of Lyon. It is known that Eucherius cited Theodorus as his source for the story of the Theban legion. Eucherius used the story to encourage his contemporary Christians serving in the Roman army to ignore the orders of their pagan superiors and instead side with the Christians. The dissemination of the story was successful in drawing pilgrims to Abbey of Saint-Maurice d'Agaune. The institution was created ex nihilo from 515 onwards by Sigismund, the first Catholic king of the Burgundians. The abbey was unique in its time as the creation of a king working in concord with bishops, rather than an organic development that occurred around the central figure of a holy monk. The new abbey was without a doubt strengthened by the strong founding legend.

Documentation
Records indicate Theodorus was appointed to be the bishop of Octodurum in present day Martigny, Switzerland. He is known to have participated in the Council of Aquileia in 381, his presence being preserved on the attendance list as "Theodorus Episcopus Octodorensis." Theodorus was also one of the signatories of a letter addressed by the Synod of Milan to Pope Siricius early in 390, informing him of their condemnation of the monk Jovinian and his followers.

In the 6th century Octodurus became unsafe because of massive migrations. As a result, the bishop's seat was moved to the fortified town of Sion, Switzerland. The bones of Theodorus were transported to the new site and later exhibited in a burial niche. This burial niche, an arched grave similar to a sarcophagus, was rediscovered in the early 1960s by excavations in the crypt under Saint Theodorus's Church in Sion.

Centuries after his death, many relics of Theodorus wound up in the fortified Valeria Church in Switzerland. Unfortunately, they were lost to the plundering of French troops during the French Revolution.

<u>Popularity</u>
Although Theodorus was a popular figure in life, for a time his legend grew in death, especially during the middle Ages in Switzerland and the Savoy region of France.

In the 8th century, German-speaking Walsers who had migrated into the canton of Valais in Switzerland were particularly devoted to the saint. In the 13th century when many Walsers left the Wallis region and spread to Italy, Liechtenstein, and Austria, they took the legend of Theodorus with them. They dedicated altars and bells to him, founded eternal seasons in his honor, and erected statues of him.

Today the adoration of Theodorus is found not only in the canton of Valais and among the Walsers but in the rest of Switzerland and throughout northern Italy, France, southern Germany, Liechtenstein, and Austria. The festival of Saint Theodorus is celebrated in parts of Europe on August 16.

In 1981, a postage stamp was issued by Liechtenstein to commemorate the 1600 year anniversary of Theodorus's appointment to the post of bishop. The horizontal stamp depicts a sculpture of Theodorus from the parish church of Laterns. The approximately 500-year-old sculpture is thought to be among the most beautiful visual images of the saint. The stamp was designed by Bruno Kaufmann and Walter Wachter.

Origin of the surname

Joder Huebel -- German for "Yoder Hill" -- is a natural fortress on the Emme River in the Swiss Canton of Berne. German researcher Karl Joder of Ludwigshafen am Rhein believes that the Yoder family was established in the region surrounding the hill before recorded history. The oldest known documentation of the Yoder family is a 1260 record of the birth of a Peter Joder in Joder Huebel. Thus, the first Yoders emerged between the start of Theodorus's reign near 381 and 1260 when the earliest records document the existence of a Yoder.

In about 1385, a Heini Joder moved to Steffisburg, Switzerland, which is in the southern part of the Emmental. Yoders lived in Steffisburg for approximately eleven generations before they joined the politically subversive Anabaptists.

Diaspora

Yoders were a part of the great German migration to America between 1650 and 1730 when Yost Yoder moved to Bucks County, PA. When the Quaker William Penn established the colony of Pennsylvania, he opened it to all religious faiths, allowing complete religious freedom and worship. He sent agents into the Rhine Valley and the Rhineland-Palatinate announcing the opportunities for settlement in his colony and assuring emigrants they would be allowed freedom of worship. Germans of all faiths came to the new colony by the thousands. They found their way down the Rhine River to Rotterdam, the great Dutch port, and embarked on slow sailing boats for Philadelphia. Between 1700 and 1775 more than sixty thousand Germans came to America. Some ethnic Germans from the Duchy of Baden, Alsace (Elsass) and Switzerland also left Europe at French ports like Le Havre.

After taking the oath of allegiance to the English Crown, the Germans spread out into the area of southeastern Pennsylvania, looking for good land and places to make their

7

new homes. They settled first in what are now Bucks, Montgomery, Chester, Lancaster, and Berks Counties. Many Yoders were among these early German pioneers. Yoder is a very common surname among the Amish and Mennonites.

Notes from the author:
Our own Amish ancestors arrived in the Philadelphia port on Sept 11, 1742.

In Summary, prior to 12th century Europe, people had given names but not surnames. To distinguish one from the other people were referred to as "Joseph son of John" or maybe Joseph the smith, etc. After a period of several centuries, these "distinguishing names" became surnames.

Saint Theodorus was considered a great and a good man and had many followers and admirers. These people became known as "Joders" and eventually this became their surname.

The earliest recorded Joder was about 1260. This is probably because they had just recently taken this as a surname.

Chapter 2
European Yoder Ancestry

Yoder Chapel in Switzerland

The reader should keep in mind that the following information is largely unproven. Links may or may not be correct. The information up to Casper Yoder(Y) was pieced together from various sources by the author and is unproven. The ancestors are shown in descending order, oldest to youngest. (Y) is the designation for European Yoders (Joders) as opposed to the designation "YR" for American Yoders found in later chapters.

Peter Joder was born in Joder Huebel near Eggiwill in 1260. He married Verena Habegger.

Casper Joder was born in 1300 in Joder Huebel. Casper was married to Veronica Dreyer.

Ulli Joder was born in 1340 in Joder Huebel and was married to Elsi Zaug (Zook).

Heini Joder was born 1365 in Joder Huebel, Bern, Switzerland and was married Lemi Gerber.

Jost Joder was born 1387 in Huttwil, Bern, Switzerland. He was married to Madiene Schluecter.

Casper Joder married Anni Meyer. Nothing else is known about Casper.

Casper Joder was born 1484 in Steffisburg, Bern, Switzerland. Casper was married to Margret Moser.

Balthasar Joder was born 1525 in Steffisburg, Bern, Switzerland and was married to Anna Roth.

Kasper Joder was born 1548 Steffisburg, Bern, Switzerland. Married Margaretha Moser Jan 17, 1571.

Casper Joder (Y) born 24 Feb 1571 Steffisburg, Bern, Switzerland. Married Margreth Hennig July 14, 1596.

Jost Joder (Y6) born 20 Nov 1607 Bern, Switzerland. He married Anna Trachsel Oct 14, 1642.

      Hans (Y61)
      Anna (Y62)
      Verena (Y63)

Peter (Y64)
Jacob (Y65)
Anna (Y66)
Barbara (Y67)
Christian (Y68)
Anna (Y69)
Jost (Y6a)
Casper (Y6b)
Cathi (Y6c)

Jost (Y6), proven through DNA testing by *YNL*, is certain to be the grandfather of our ancestors YR1 and YR2. Any one of his six sons could have been the father of our ancestors, with the exception of Casper. Since all of Casper's sons remained in Germany it is unlikely that he is the "unknown" father.

While it is probable that the other Joders listed here are related ancestors, any link prior to Jost (Y6) is very speculative.

Chapter 3
Our Amish Divergence

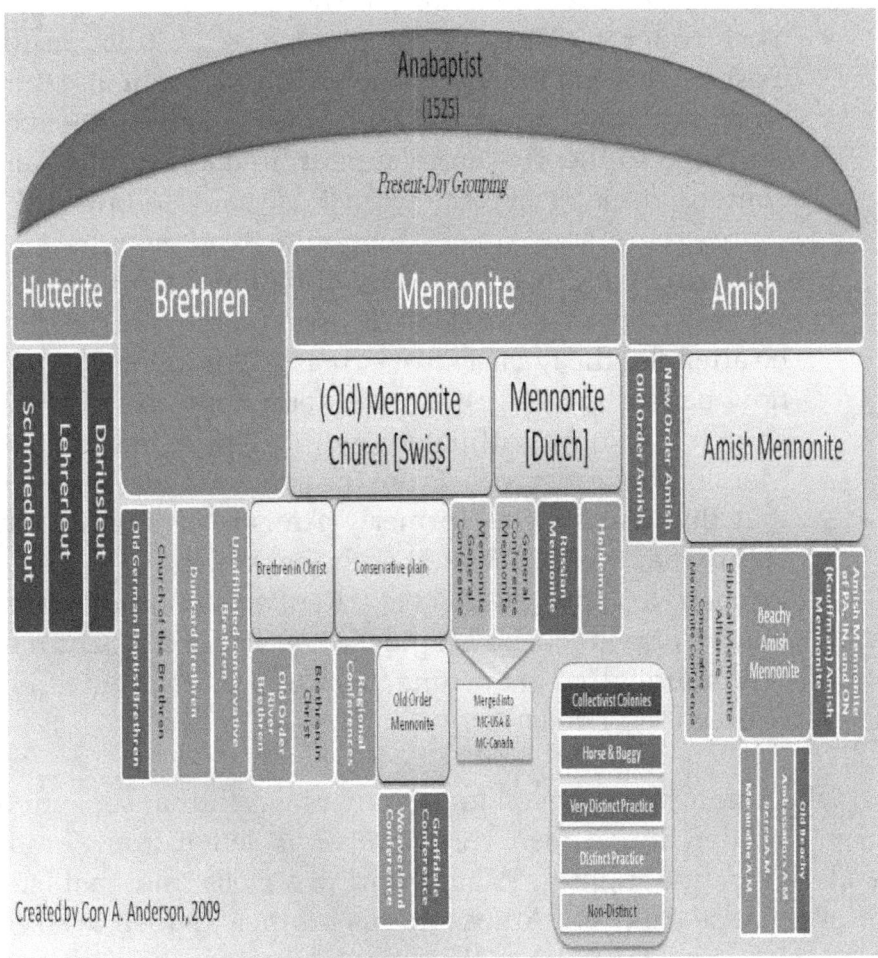

The figure shows a classification diagram of Anabaptist groups.

Anabaptist (1525)

Present-Day Grouping

Hutterite | Brethren | Mennonite | Amish

Schmiedeleut, Lehrerleut, Dariusleut

(Old) Mennonite Church [Swiss] | Mennonite [Dutch]

New Order Amish | Old Order Amish | Amish Mennonite

Old German Baptist Brethren, Church of the Brethren, Dunkard Brethren, Unaffiliated conservative Brethren, Brethren in Christ, Conservative plain

Mennonite General Conference, General Conference Mennonite, Russian Mennonite, Holdeman

Biblical Mennonite Alliance, Conservative Mennonite Conference, Beachy Amish Mennonite, Amish Mennonite of PA, IN, and ON [Kauffman] Amish Mennonite

Old Order River Brethren, Brethren in Christ, Regional Conferences, Old Order Mennonite, Merged into MC-USA & MC-Canada, Collectivist Colonies, Horse & Buggy, Very Distinct Practice, Distinct Practice, Non-Distinct

Weaverland Conference, Groffdale Conference

Maranatha A. M., Ambassadors A. M., Sermon A. M., Old Beachy

Created by Cory A. Anderson, 2009

It is well documented that at least the first three of our Yoder immigrant ancestors were Amish.

- Christian Yoder YR2 – While Christian's father is unproven, the speculated father was probably an Amish minister.
- John (Hans) Yoder YR25 – We have little information about John. However, considering that both his son and

13

his father were documented Amish, it is unrealistic to believe that he was not.

- John (Jotter Hannes) Yoder YR251 - He has been documented to be an Amish bishop.
- Yost Yoder YR2511 – While the Church affiliation for Yost and his son John is unknown, it is thought that they were probably a part of the Amish community that migrated to the Tuscarora area of Juniata County. This community later became extinct as many followed the more progressive Amish Mennonite to other areas.
- John Yoder YR25111 - Church affiliation is unknown.
- Moses P. Yoder YR251114 – Moses' obituary states that he attended the Locust Grove *Amish* Mennonite Church, now named the Locust Grove Mennonite Church. This church is now affiliated with The Conservative Mennonite Conference. From the previous chart you see that this church was formerly Amish Mennonite and before that it was affiliated with the Amish.
- Reuben K. Yoder YR2511144 – Reuben's obituary states that he attended The Maple Grove Mennonite Church. It is thought that at the time this was a more progressive church than Locust Grove.

So who amongst our seven grandfathers was it that separated from and left the Amish community? A letter from Amos Yoder's granddaughter, Mary Marlowe, tells me that she thinks that as children, Amos and his brother Reuben dressed as Amish. She speculates that maybe it was the industry coming to Belleville that drew them from the Amish community. However, after reading many documents and reading the history of the Amish and Mennonites, it becomes clear that there have been many schisms and differences among these groups. I leave it to others to explain why this occurred. So, while I still can't identify where our line left the Amish community, I don't believe that it was an individual who left, but rather a congregation, and that it wasn't an event as much as a migration or evolution. The charts explain and simplify some of the migration that has occurred. The charts were copied from The Beachy Amish website: http://www.beachyam.org/amishmennonites.htm.

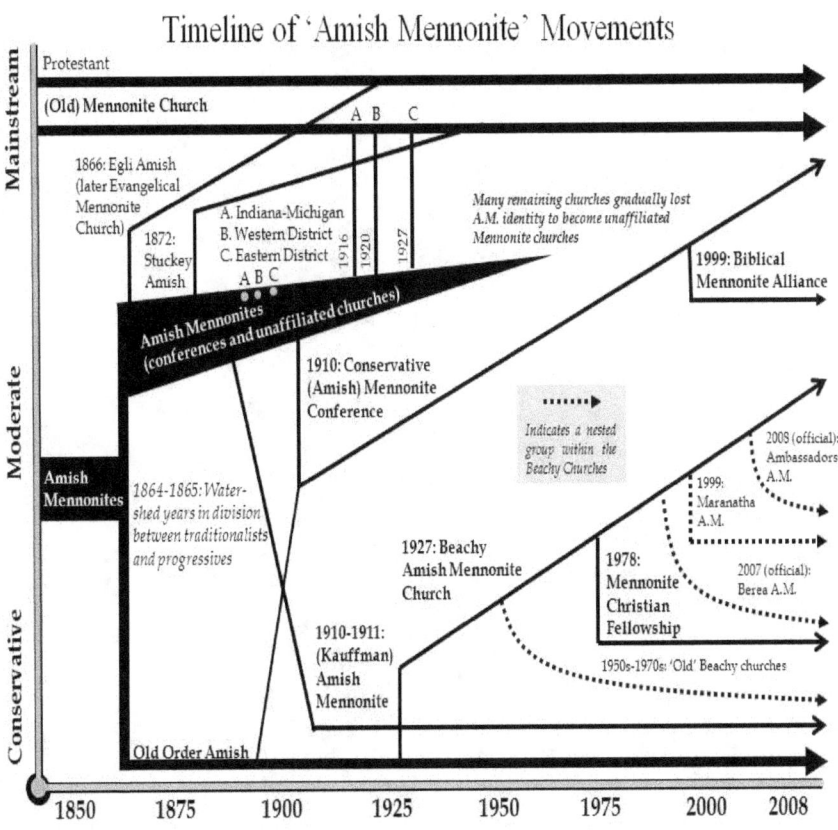

Timeline of 'Amish Mennonite' Movements

Generation 1

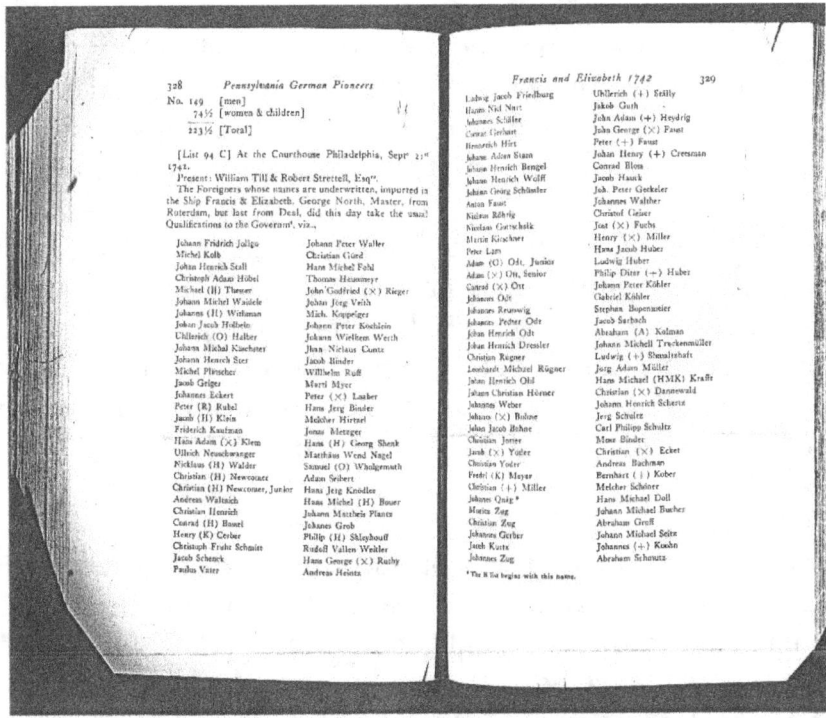

Ship's List of First Amish Yoder Immigrants

In the following chapters, I have attempted to use the same numbering scheme as that used in *Amish and Amish Mennonite Genealogies (AAMG)* to identify individuals. You will see numbers like YR251. This number would signify, starting on the right, the first child of the fifth child of the second child, etc. YR is the designation for American Amish Yoders. (The author's reference number would be YR251114423)

Our first American generation ancestor was Christian Yoder YR2. Before discussing him and his family, we first need to provide some discussion about his brother YR1 and his family. We do not know the name of the brother; hence, we can only reference him as YR1. It is known that he was born in 1695 and five years older than YR2; therefore, the designation YR1. I include this reference to YR1's family in order to highlight the confusion one might encounter if researching our family. Both YR1 and YR2 were married to women named Barbara. YR1 either died or was lost at sea on his journey to America. Since YR1's name is not known and the last name of his wife Barbara also is not known, lore refers to her as "Widow Barbara".

As if having wives with the same name is not confusing enough, YR1 had nine children and YR2 had eight children. Six of the children in each family had the same given names. All children of both families were born in Europe and both families immigrated to America on the same ship. Young children and women were apparently not listed on the ship's log.

1. **Christian Yoder[1] YR2**
   Christian was born in Europe around 1700 and was married to a woman named Barbara, last name unknown. This marriage produced eight children, all of which were believed to have been born in Europe.
   (Note: Highlighted print designates our direct ancestors)
   > 2a. Barbara Yoder b: 1725
   > 2b. Magdalena Yoder b: 1726
   > 2c. Christian Yoder b: 1728 d: 11/20/1816
   > 2d. Elizabeth Yoder b: 1729 d: 9/1/1771
   > **2e. John Yoder[2] b: 1732 d: 7/2/1813**
   > 2f. Yost Yoder b: 1734
   > 2g. Veronica Yoder b: 1738
   > 2h. Jacob Yoder b: 1740

Christian YR2 and Barbara, along with their eight children, immigrated to America on Sept 11, 1742, aboard the ship *Francis & Elizabeth*. The ship's master was George North. The ship originated in Rotterdam, Holland, and stopped at Deal, England, along the way.

While there are several possibilities, the father of YR1 and YR2 is unknown. Extensive research has been done in this area, especially by the *Yoder Newsletter* (YNL). The YNL has sponsored DNA testing of several branches of Yoders. They have also paid a professional researcher to comb the archives in Switzerland. Several noted professors have also researched this link in Switzerland and Germany. The DNA research takes them the closest. It is strongly believed that Yost Joder Y6 and Anna Trachsel were the grandparents of YR1 and our ancestor Christian YR2.

Yost Y6 and Anna had twelve children, six sons and six daughters. Although it is possible that any one of the sons could be the father of YR1 and YR2, Chris Yoder at the YNL believes that Casper Y6b can be ruled out because all of his sons stayed in Germany. Yost was an Amish minister. Again it should be stressed that no matter what we see published, the father of YR2 at this writing is not definitely known.

Christian and Barbara traveled from the arrival port of Philadelphia to Berks County, where there was already an established Amish community. Christian individually, and also with his son Jacob, applied for land patents to Thomas and Richard Penn, sons of William Penn. Warrants were approved in 1757 and patents were granted in 1765 and 1766 (See Appendix 8). It is not known where they lived while waiting for these patents to be issued; however, it was not unusual for people to occupy and use land until they accumulated enough money to apply for a patent. The land was not free.

The home and barn built on these lands still stands today. The address is 2652 Tilden Rd., Mohrsville, PA 19954.

It is believed that Christian and Barbara are buried in the Northkill Cemetery. Unfortunately, there are no records and the headstones have long been obliterated. The AAMG believes that Christian may have been an Amish Bishop at the time of his death.

Home of Christian YR2 & Barbara Yoder in Berks County

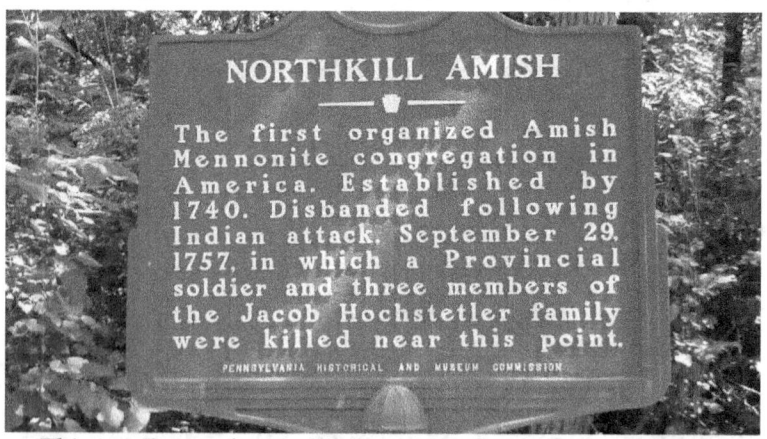

NORTHKILL AMISH

The first organized Amish Mennonite congregation in America. Established by 1740. Disbanded following Indian attack, September 29, 1757, in which a Provincial soldier and three members of the Jacob Hochstetler family were killed near this point.

PENNSYLVANIA HISTORICAL AND MUSEUM COMMISSION

This is a Pennsylvania historical marker found behind the Roadside America building along I78 near Reading PA.

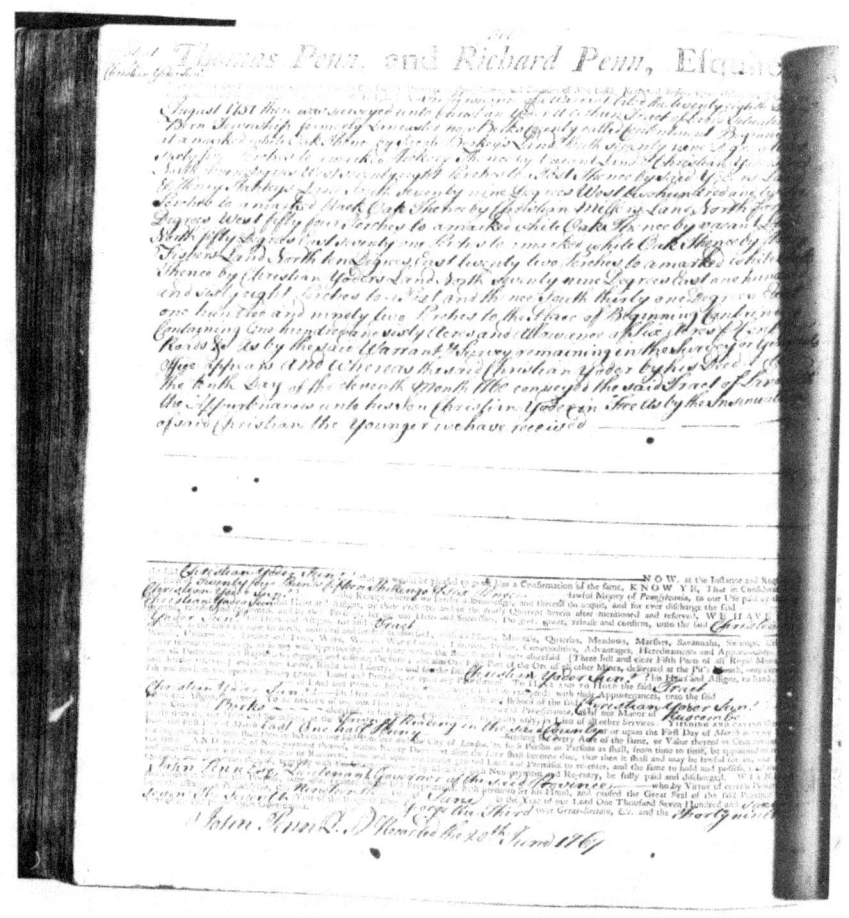

Land Patent from Thomas & Richard Penn (Children of William Penn) To
Christian Yoder YR2 (Also see appendix 8)

Generation 2

2e. John "Hans" Yoder[2] YR25 (Christian[1])

John was born in Europe in 1732. He died on July 2, 1813 in Mifflin County. He married Anna Mast, born in 1734. Together they produced eight children.

3a. John Yoder[3] b: 1754
3b. Magdalena Yoder b: 7/9/1761
3c. Jacob Yoder b: 7/17/1763
3d. Barbara Yoder b: 1765 d: April 1836
3e. Anna Yoder b: 1770
3f. Christian Yoder b: 1774 d: 12/19/1827
3g. Yost Yoder b: abt 1775 d: 1856
3h. Veronica Yoder b: 1779 d: 12/31/1827

John moved to Mifflin County soon after his son Bishop John moved to Milroy. It is not known exactly when he moved but the book "Mifflin County Amish and Mennonite Story" by Duane Kauffman shows Tax Lists of 1794 in which John is shown to own 300 acres on a deed also dated 1794.

John & Anna's log home still stands in Mifflin County along Coffee Run about two miles north of The Woolen Mills. It sets over a large spring that Penn State researchers had determined to originate in the mountains several miles away.

Home of John "Hans" YR25 and Anna Yoder
Along Coffee Run in Mifflin County

Generation 3

3a. Bishop John (Jotter Hannes) Yoder[3] YR251 (John (Hans[2]), Christian[1])

John seemed to have wanderlust. He was born in Berks County, PA in 1754. He moved to Somerset County, PA in 1775, Mifflin County in 1791, Centre County in 1805, and finally to Wayne County, Ohio in 1826. The date of his death is unknown.

John married Barbara Richenbach. Barbara was born in 1755 in Lancaster County, PA; the date of her death is also unknown. Together they had nine children.

> **4a. Yost Yoder[4] b: 7/27/1775 d: 5/3/1849**
> 4b. Jacob Yoder[4] b: abt1779 d: abt1852
> 4c. Magdalena Yoder[4]
> 4d. Christian Yoder[4] b: 8/?/1784 d: 5/3/1850
> 4e. Anna Yoder[4] b: 3/10/1786 d: 6/18/1877
> 4f. Barbara Yoder[4] b: 2/10/1788 d: 1/6/1870
> 4g. Daniel Yoder[4] b: 4/21/1792 d: 12/1/1882
> 4h. John Yoder[4]
> 4i. Elizabeth Yoder[4] b: 4/13/1799 d: 5/8/1890

It is thought that John was a Minister when he left Berks County in 1775. There seemed to be trouble within the church in this period causing large migrations. In 1791, John left Somerset County for Milroy in Mifflin County. A copy of the original purchase agreement between John and Henry Milroy is found in Appendix 9. The purchase was for 212 acres and contained a large stone house. The house is beautiful and still stands today at the end of King St. in Milroy. Initials "JBY" (John Barbara Yoder) are found under the eaves of the roof on one end of the house.

John left Mifflin County in 1805 and moved to Half-Moon Valley in Centre County and from there to Wayne County, Ohio where he served as Bishop in the Amish community.

The MCA&MS has a Table titled "First Decade Amish Residents of Mifflin County". This list shows that John was in the 1800 census and was on the county tax rolls.

1791 Yoder & Milroy Agreement

Articles of agreement made and concluded by and between Henry Milroy of Armagh Township, Mifflin County and state of Pennsylvania of the one part and John Yoter [sic] of Brothers Valley Township, Bedford County and state aforesaid of the other part witnesseth that the above named Henry Milroy hath granted, bargained, and sold all that certain tract of land whereupon he now liveth in Armagh Township containing two hundred and twelve acres with the usual allowances unto the above named John Yoter for the sum of seven hundred and ten pounds to be paid in the manner and form following viz: Two hundred and fifty pounds to be paid on the first day of May insuing and the remainder or residue of four hundred and sixty pounds in seven equal payments, one to be made on the first day of May, Seventeen Hundred and Ninety Two and one on the first day of May in each year untill [sic] the whole be paid. The said John Yoter is to have peaceable possession of the premises when the first payment is made excepting one room and part of another in the mansion house together with a weaver shop which the above named Henry Milroy is to have the privilege of occupying with his family untill the first day of May Seventeen Hundred and Ninety Two. The above named Henry Millroy [sic] also reserves the crop of rye that is now growing on the premises and all the wheat that is sowed on new ground together with the crop of grass that is now growing on the new meadow which crops he shall be allowed the privilege of cuting, [sic] securing, and using on the premises without interruption but if he moves off the plantation before time of mowing he is not to sell the grass. The above named Henry Milroy immediately upon the above named John Yoter's paying him the first payment of two hundred and fifty pounds is to convey the above said tract of land to said John Yoter. He is also to patent one hundred and ninety six acres of the above named tract of land against the time of the first payment and the remaining sixteen acres before the second payment mentioned above and for the true performance of the above agreement each of the above named parties do bind themselves and their heirs with the other in the just and full sum of one thousand two hundred and twenty pounds lawful money. In testimony whereof each of the above named parties with their respective hands and seals this Sixteenth day of March One thousand Seven hundred and Ninety One.

Henry Milroy   John Yoder

Signed, sealed and delivered in the presence of
James Johnston   Johannes Zuig [sic]
Mifflin County, Pa.

Before the subscriber one of the associate judges for said county came James Johnston and was sworn as law directs that he was personally present and saw Henry Milroy deceased and John Yoter sign, seal, and deliver the within testament of writing and that his name as a witness was his own respective hand writing and saw John Suke [sic] the other subscriber being witness sign his name thereto as a witness.

Sworn and subscribed November 8, 1792   James Johnston
Before William Brown

Recorded 8th November 1792 and compared with the original
Samuel Johnston

This document was taken from *Mifflin County Amish and Mennonite Story* 1791-1991 by S. Duane Kauffman. It is a transcription of the original longhand copy found in Appendix 9.

This is the Milroy, Mifflin County home of Bishop John (Jotter Hannes) YR251 and Barbara Yoder. It sets at the end of King Street in Milroy. In it, in the parlor, is found a metal gunpowder storage cabinet and the outer walls contain gun turrets. At the time of this writing, it was being restored by the current owners.

Generation 4

4a. Yost Yoder[4] YR2511 (Bishop John[3], John (Hans[2]), Christian[1])

Little information is found regarding Yost Yoder. He was born on July 27, 1775 in Berks County, PA. He traveled with or followed his family through Somerset, Mifflin and Centre Counties, finally settling in Juniata County. Yost was married to Sarah Yoder (YR1252) b: 9/11/1776 d: 5/6/1844. This union produced sixteen (16) children. The first ten were born in Mifflin County, the last five in Centre County. It is unknown where Sarah, the eleventh, child was born. Yost died in Juniata County on 5/3/1849 at the age of 73. He was probably our most prolific ancestor.

    5a. John H. Yoder[5] b: 1/12/1800 d: 5/25/1867
    5b. Daniel Yoder[5] b:
    5c. Jacob Yoder[5] b:
    5d. Elizabeth Yoder[5] b: 2/16/1803 d: 5/1/1885
    5e. Veronica Yoder[5] b: 2/14/1804 d: 4/17/1874
        (Fanny)
    5f. Barbara Yoder[5] b: 6/27/1805 d: 8/14/1883
    5g. Susanna Yoder[5] b: 9/19/1806 d: 6/16/1893
    5h. Christian Yoder[5] b: 6/9/1809 d: 12/23/1848
    5i. Magdalena Yoder[5] b: 9/30/1810 d: 8/16/1883
    5j. Leah Yoder[5] b: 11/9/1811 d: 7/6/1888
    5k. Sarah Yoder[5] b: 1/16/1813 d: 4/26/1846
    5l. Joseph Yoder[5] b: 6/14/1814 d: 12/24/1898
    5m. Daniel Yoder[5] b: 3/4/1816 d: 3/23/1896 (Grey Dan)
    5n. Moses Yoder[5] b: 3/4/1816 d: 1818
    5o. Rachel Yoder[5] b: 4/2/1817 d: 8/21/1897
    5p. Stephen Yoder[5] b: 1/4/1821 d: 7/22/1908

Generation 5

5a. John H. Yoder[5] YR25111 (Yost[4], Bishop John[3], John (Hans[2]), Christian[1])

Home of John H & Veronica Yoder and possibly the home of his father and mother, Yost and Sarah Yoder. The home is found in Spruce Hill Township, Juniata County in an area called Half-Moon.

John was born on Jan 12, 1800 in Mifflin County. He was married twice. His first marriage was to Salome Yoder (YR1619?). This union produced three children.

    6a. Sarah Yoder b: 5/20/1830 d: 7/1/1910
    6b. Catherine Yoder b: 2/19/1833 d: 2/18/1898
    6c. Isaiah Yoder b: 12/28/1835 d: 7/20/1925

John's second marriage was to Veronica (Fanny) Kauffman (KF3325) b: 1/26/1813 d: 1/6/1892. This marriage produced nine children.

    6d. Moses P Yoder[6] b: 8/17/1839 d: 11/27/1910
    6e. Mary Yoder abt 1841
    6f. Elizabeth Yoder[6] abt 1842
    6g. Lydia Yoder b: 4/23/1844 d: 1/9/1933
    6h. Joseph Yoder[6] b: 1/1/1847 d: 4/15/1929
    6i. John Yoder[6] b: 5/23/1849 d??
    6j. Rebecca Yoder[6] b: 1/22/1855 d: 3/11/1891

6k. Anna D. Yoder[6] b: 10/16/1857 d: 12/16/1923
6l. Salina Yoder[6] b: 5/25/1860 d: 1/10/1916

John died on May 26, 1867. Although he left three young daughters, John had a very detailed will (partially shown in Appendix 10) that provided specific instructions for their care. Moses P. was named executor. It is believed that both Moses and his brother Joseph purchased parts of John H.'s property. An exhaustive inventory of his personal effects is found in his probate in the Juniata County courthouse.

John and Fanny are shown in the 1850 (Appendix 3) census in Turbett Township, Juniata County, PA. (Locally, this area is known as Half Moon.) His three children from his first marriage were living with them, as well as six children from his second marriage. His occupation was listed as farmer with real estate worth $5500.

In the 1860 census John and Fanny are shown in Spruce Hill Township, Juniata County, PA. He was still listed as a farmer with real estate worth $8000 and personal property worth $2000. (The homestead locations of Turbett Township and Spruce Hill Township are one and the same. Sometime between these two censuses, Turbett was split and Spruce Hill was formed.)

Generation 6

6d. Moses P. Yoder[6] YR251114 (John H[5], Yost[4], Bishop John[3], John (Hans[2]), Christian[1])

Remains in Spruce Hill, Juniata Co   Home near Belleville, PA
Homesteads of Moses P. and Sarah Yoder

Moses was born on Aug 17, 1839 in Spruce Hill Township, Juniata County, Pennsylvania and died Nov 27, 1910 in Mifflin County, Pennsylvania. Moses was married to Sarah Byler, daughter of Bishop Solomon and Sarah (Hertzler) Byler. Sarah was born on Nov 21, 1843 and died on Feb 19, 1923. This union produced two sons and two daughters. Both Moses and Sarah's obituaries say that they were faithful members of the Locust Grove Amish Mennonite Church, and that both were of a friendly disposition.

Sarah (Byler) Yoder with granddaughter
Arvilla at the homestead in Belleville

7a. Emma E. Yoder[7], b: Dec 24, 1869 d: Sept 15, 1903
7b. Amos E. Yoder[7,] b: July 11, 1871 d: Sept 21, 1968

33

7c. Sallie M. Yoder[7,] b: Feb 16, 1874 d: May 3, 1912*
7d. Reuben K. Yoder[7], b: Oct 1, 1880 d: June 11, 1958

The 1850 census showed Moses being 11 years old and living with his parents in Turbot Township, Juniata County, PA.

1863 land records of Spruce Hill, Juniata County, Pennsylvania show property owned by John H. Yoder, father of Moses P. His will names four tracts totaling over 200 acres. It is assumed that some, if not all, of the land was inherited or purchased from the estate of his father Yost.

The 1870 census showed Moses as the head of household with his wife Sarah and his daughter Emma, six months of age. The location is shown as Spruce Hill Township, Juniata County, PA. (Spruce Hill was split off from Turbot in 1858) Moses' occupation was listed as farmer, his real estate valued at $4000, and personal effects at $1000.

An 1877 land map shows the same land now split, with Moses P. owning part of that land and the other part still owned by his Father John H., even though John H. had died in 1867. In John H.'s will, Moses was named executor. This same will directs Moses to sell the land one year or more after his death. It is assumed that Moses bought some of this land from the estate of his father John.

The 1880 census showed Moses and Sarah living in Union Township, Mifflin County, PA. His occupation was shown as Farmer. Their children Emma 10, Amos 8, and Sally 6 were with them and Emma was attending school. Sarah's mother and father, Solomon and Sally Byler, were apparently also living with them. They were respectively 81 and 80 years of age. There was also a James Manbeck living with them and he was listed as a laborer. He was assumed to work as a hired hand for Moses.

34

The 1890 census records were destroyed in a fire at the national archives.

In the 1900 census, Moses and Sarah were still living in Union Township with only their daughter Sallie, 16, living with them. At this point, Moses listed his occupation as "Landlord".

The 1910 census showed Moses and Sarah still living in Union Township. This census also showed their son Reuben, 30, again living with them. On the previous census, they listed their residence as a farm; however, on this census they list it as a home. Moses' occupation says "Due Insurance". Since Social Security did not begin until 1945 it is assumed to mean that he was retired and living on some other kind of insurance.

Civil War Draft Registrations (Appendix 5) show that Moses was drafted but had a substitute serving in his place.

The book *Mifflin County Amish and Mennonite Story* by Duane Kauffman states that several "Amish & Amish Mennonite" bought 30 or more shares of KV Railroad stock at $25 a share. The book *The Ol' Hook & Eye* confirms that Moses was one of the larger stockholders with 48 shares. This book also lists Moses as a Director of the railroad. The probate of his will showed that he still owed $378.90 for this stock at the time of his death.

The book *Mifflin County Amish and Mennonite Story* lists Union Township grain growers (1879 Wheat and 1880 Corn) and it shows that Moses P. grew 991 bushels of wheat & oats on 35 acres and 1300 bushels of corn on 12 acres.

*Moses' daughter Sallie was married to Thomas E. Zook of the partnership of the Hartzler & Zook Foundry Company in Belleville.

Generation 7
Reuben Kauffman Yoder YR2511144
Mary Mae Zook ZK216397

7d. Reuben K. (Hicks) Yoder[7] (Moses P[6], John H[5], Yost[4], Bishop John[3], John (Hans[2]), Christian[1])

Reuben was born in Union Township, Mifflin County, Pennsylvania on Oct 1, 1880. Reuben died on June 11, 1958 in the Lewistown Hospital of cerebral hemorrhage.

Mary Mae Zook[6] (Solomon[5], David[4], Abraham[3], John[2], Moritz[1]) was born near Allensville, Mifflin County, Pennsylvania on May 2, 1888 and died at a nursing home in Mifflintown, PA on April 5, 1969.

Reuben and Mary were married on July 20, 1911. They attended the Maple Grove Mennonite Church and both are buried in the Locust Grove Mennonite cemetery.

Reuben and Mary had seven children.

8a. Alta Z. Yoder[8] YR25111441, Jan 18, 1912 – Jan 20, 1912

8b. Elton "Hicks" Saul Yoder[8] YR25111442, March 12, 1914 – Jan 19, 1972
m. Aug 11, 1934 to Verdie Irene Pearson, July 25, 1913 – June 22, 2009

8c. Elmer David Yoder[8], YR25111443 May 14, 1915 – Oct 27, 1993
m. to Winifred B Wilson

8d. Arvilla Mae Yoder[8] YR25111444, March 10, 1917 – July 17, 2011
m. April 5, 1942 to Trennis Samuel King, April 8, 1917 – April 16, 2002

8e. Pauline Clare Yoder[8] YR25111445, Nov 5, 1920 – March 10, 2006
m. April 1, 1944 to Paul Leonard King, April 1, 1920 – June 3, 1970

8f. Lola Lorraine Yoder[8] YR25111446, July 8, 1925 – April 12, 1990
m. Charles Goss

8g. Merle Roy Yoder[8] YR25111447, Oct 2, 1926 – Feb 14, 2006
m1. to Arlene Crownover
m2. Aug 30, 1969 to Elizabeth J. Bloss

8h. Lucille Marian Yoder[8] YR25111448, Oct 7, 1930 – Aug 4, 2012
m. July 7, 1951 to Robert Schueck Gotwals, July 12, 1929

Reuben was the fourth child of Moses P. Yoder (YR251114) and Sarah Byler.
Reuben's siblings were;

Emma E. b: 12/24/1869
Amos E. b: 7/11/1871
Sallie M. b: 2/16/1874

All of the siblings were born in Spruce Hill Township, Juniata County, Pennsylvania.

Reuben appears in census records for years 1900, 1910, 1920, 1930 & 1940. Most 1890 census records were destroyed in a fire.

Reuben (left of cook) at Kish Camp near Greenwood Furnace

Mary appears in the census records 1900 & 1910 with her family, then with Reuben in years 1920, 1930 & 1940.

Arvilla, Lola & Elmer

In the 1900 census year, Reuben was living in Union Township with his brother Amos and his brother's wife Lydia. He was shown as being 19 years old and born in Oct 1880. He was listed as a farm laborer, as having gone to school and as being able to read and write. The number of years of school was not provided. Amos' occupation was listed as farmer so it is assumed that Reuben worked for his brother.

In the 1900 census, Mary was shown in Union Township with her parents, born in May 1888, 12 years old and in school.

In the 1910 census Reuben was still living in Union Township but he was living in the same household as his father Moses and mother Sarah. It says that he was 30 years old and was now a machinist. He most probably worked for the Hartzler & Zook machine Company. No occupation was listed for his father.

Elmer, Arvilla & Elton

In the 1910 census Mary was still at home with her family, she was 22 years old and occupation was listed as a nurse.

Reuben and Mary were married on July 20, 1911. They lived in Belleville, PA. Their marriage license (see appendix 6) was dated July 18, 1911. It indicated that Reuben was 30 years old and that he was a machinist. The license said that Mary was 23 years old and her occupation was seamstress.

In 1918 Reuben registered for the Selective Service Draft for World War I (see appendix 5). Maybe it should be noted that Reuben's father Moses P was registered for the Civil War, was drafted, but had a "substitute server". That was in 1863.

Pauline & Arvilla

The 1920 census record brought Reuben and Mary together. The record shows them living in Union Township with three children, Elton, Elmer and Arvilla. It states that they owned their home free of a mortgage. No address was given. The record shows that Reuben was now the Employer/Proprietor of a coal yard.

The 1930 census shows Reuben and Mary still in Union Township but this time specifically in Belleville. They have added three children, Pauline, Lola and Merle. It still shows Reuben as the owner of a coal yard and says that he was not a veteran.

The 1940 census now puts them on Walnut St. in Belleville. This record shows the value of their home to be $5,000 and Arvilla was still living at home and was working as a telephone operator. Elton and Elmer have now moved out of the house. Elton was shown at a different address with his family.

There are many references to Reuben and also pictures of The Yoder Coal Yard in the book "The Ol' Hook & Eye" by John G. Hartzler. It indicates that Reuben bought the coal yard from Samuel A. Hostetler in August of 1916. This book tells that by 1920, Reuben was going through three train car loads of coal a week. It says that if he received a carload on Saturday, he had it sold by Monday. These cars were apparently shoveled out by hand until 1931 when James A. Stuter & Sons built an elevated tipple for emptying the coal cars. Another part of the book states that in 1931, Reuben was delivering coal directly from the mines to the customer. Sometimes my Dad would take me along to the mines in Shamokin for a load of coal. I also remember going along to help deliver coal to people's homes. I don't remember connecting the two events but I do remember that it was hard work and my "helping" was mostly just standing around watching.

Another part of the book says that on Sunday, April 19, 1925 a tornado struck the coal yard. The office, scale house, coal sheds and feed building were completely "mashed to the ground".

The book says that soon after the KV Railroad stopped running, the coal yard went out of business. I am skeptical of this as when I left Belleville in 1953, the business was still operational. Probably like his competitor, The Belleville Grain Elevator, Reuben was most likely moving coal directly from the mines to the consumer. The scales were dismantled in the 1970's.

(r)Elmer & Elton
(f)Pauline & Arvilla

There is a card from 1942 (see appendix 5) showing that Reuben registered for the draft for World War II. This card also lists their address as Walnut St, Belleville. It states that he was born on Oct 1, 1880. He was 61 years old, 5'11" tall, weighted 160 pounds, had brown eyes, black hair and a ruddy complexion. This record also states that their telephone number was "35-R-11".

Reuben's nickname was "Hicks". Nobody seems to know where this came from but an older Belleville resident told me that everybody in the family acquired the name. I was told that in high school even Lucy was affectionately called "Lucy Hicks".

42

Memories of the Grandchildren

Memories from Donna (Yoder) Henninger

I am going to describe our grandparent's house, as I spent a lot of time there as a child. It was a large, white house that had lots of flowers and shrubs around the front porch. I especially remember the "lady slippers" as Grandma showed Lucille (Aunt Lucille, my father's youngest sister) and me how to take the flower apart and make dolls.

Entering the house from the front porch we came into a large living room and that is where the family gathered. There was a formal sitting room "parlor" through a door to the right of the living room that was used for visitors only. Grandma used to play the lap harp for us and sometimes she would allow Lucille and me to play on the "player piano". Lucille would pretend to play the piano and I would be underneath pushing the pedals. Our legs didn't reach that far! Grandpa loved to get the "marble roller" out when little grandchildren came to visit. Every now and then Grandma would have quiltings at her house. The sitting room would be filled with the quilting frame and the ladies quilting.

The door to the pantry was next to the parlor. There was always bread, pies, and cake in the pantry and it smelled so good. The telephone was on a stand beside the pantry door. To place a call, we picked up the receiver and asked for the person we were calling. Aunt Arvilla worked at the telephone exchange. I used to go and watch her while she worked and found it quite interesting.

Next to the pantry was the door to the cellar. The cellar had a coal bin, large vat for vinegar, a potato bin, cans of lard and jars of fruit and vegetables. Also, that is where the men seemed to congregate after meals. I have no idea why the men went down to the cellar because that was one place that I didn't like!

The kitchen was my favorite place because the large table was always loaded with food. It was a sunny room in which there was a wood-burning stove with a tank for hot water, a wood box, cupboards built into the wall and a dry sink. Grandma kept the table set with dishes and silverware, butter, vinegar, pickles, salt and pepper. It was covered with a white cloth between meals. I had many snacks of brown sugar sandwiches on homemade bread with lots of butter. I used to go over to a hardware store to get butter for her. At the time it seemed like just another thing to do but now I wonder why the hardware store sold butter. At holiday gatherings the men ate in the kitchen and the children at a small table in the family room while the women served the meal. When the men were finished eating they went to the cellar and the women ate. Grandma dipped hot water from the wood-burning stove when it was time to wash the dishes.

Grandma did the laundry in the summer kitchen. She was an interesting and busy person. Summer afternoons would find her on the side porch shelling peas or snapping beans. She made it look easy. Lucille and I never lasted long helping with that! She had two chores that I loved to watch her do. One was making homemade lye soap. She had a fire just outside from the summer kitchen door with a large, black cast iron kettle containing the soap over the fire. We weren't allowed to get near and I'm sure she had her hands full with Lucille and me trying to see what she was doing. She also had a fire and used a large kettle in the backyard to make apple butter. That smelled soooo good! She would put apple butter on homemade bread for us and it tasted wonderful. I thought that was right up there with the brown sugar sandwiches.

The bedrooms were upstairs. I forget how many there were, but I do remember that Grandma and Grandpa slept in a large bedroom at the front of the house. When I spent the night at their house, which was often, I slept with Lucille in the bedroom to the right of the stairs. Her bed was so high that Grandma had to boost me in. She always rubbed our foreheads and the bottoms of our feet with Vicks salve after we were on the bed. I don't know why that was done. The bathroom was between Lucille's and Mosie's (Uncle Merle, my father's youngest brother) bedrooms. It had a big bathtub with a dish containing Sweetheart soap. I thought that was wonderful!

When I spent Saturday nights at their house, I went with them to church and Sunday School on Sunday morning. After church Grandpa would take us for a little ride in the car before we went back to the house.

There was a garden behind the house with a white fence surrounding it. Grandma raised a lot of vegetables and had many types of flowers planted near the fence along with rhubarb. She canned the vegetables and shared with everyone. Nobody was allowed in the garden but Grandma. It was a big deal to "sneak" a piece of rhubarb that poked through the fence.

Grandpa was quiet. When I was about ten years old, he would have me tend the coal yard office while he went up to the house for dinner – we never called the mid-day meal lunch. Lucille, Mosie, and I spent a lot of time playing in the feed shed at Grandpa's coal yard. Mosie would push us as fast as he could between the piles of bags of feed. We'd be screaming and making so much noise that sometimes Grandpa would come over from the office to see what was going on. That's all that was needed to quiet us down!!!

My Dad, Elton, worked for Grandpa in the coal and feed business. He drove the coal truck to the coal mines in Shamokin and Phillipsburg and hauled the coal to Belleville. He then would deliver the coal to the customers. My brother, Ron, remembers riding with Dad to the mines and to deliver coal. He also hauled peas, tomatoes and green beans from farms to the cannery which was located at the top of the Reedsville hill.

We didn't have a car so Dad would bring the coal truck home on Saturday afternoon and we'd pile in and go to Lewistown. We also did a lot of visiting in the coal truck. I remember visiting Aunt Pauline and Uncle Paul at their farm and Aunt Arvilla (Sissy) and Uncle Trennis at their farm. We also visited Aunt Lola and Uncle Charlie near Lewistown. Uncle Elmer (Tuggle) and Aunt Sue lived close enough that we walked to their house to visit them. At some point in time we got an old car but it didn't last very long. We never got farther than Yeagertown without having a flat tire. Dad always had patches along and would fix it. The tire seemed to last until the next week when we got to Yeagertown!!!! Sometimes the car would stall out going through a deep water puddle and Dad would get out and crank it to get it started again.

Grandpa planted potatoes over at the farm, and the whole family helped dig and gather the potatoes. Mosie would tease us by throwing potatoes at us. The men also picked cherries at the farm when they were ripe and they would get pitted and canned. Lucille and I would spend a week during the summer at Trennis and Arvilla's farm. One time we stuffed Trennis's clothes with straw and put the "dummy" in the hired man's bed which was in the barn. It made the hired man so angry that he threatened to quit. Trennis thought it was hilarious and he never forgot the incident.

Dad raised a hog every year to be butchered. The meat was cured in my bedroom so I'd move to another room to sleep during the winter. Grandpa would share a beef with Dad and Mom. Mom canned the beef and also sausage and tenderloin from the hog. Grandpa also traded wheat for flour at the flour mill and shared that with us.

Our school sold Jello as a money-making project. That must have been after Lucille graduated from high school. When the "Jello campaign" started, I'd run all the way from school to Grandma's house for orders. She always bought at least a dozen boxes. She was my best customer!

I remember several family reunions with Grandpa's brother Amos's family from Ohio. The reunions were at a camp near Greenwood. At that time the upstairs had cots lined up in two rows the length of the building. We would spend the weekend there. The men played ball and we'd chase the balls for them. I always looked forward to "going to camp".

I also remember taking several trips to Duncansville, PA to visit Grandma's relatives. It may have been Grandma's sister. We would spend the night, and there was a girl there around the same age as Lucille. Her name was Millie. I remember that they had "banty roosters" which we were afraid of because they would chase us. The bantys would be on our heels as we ran and screamed for help. When we took that trip, it seemed like we were going to the end of the earth!!! It was a long way from Belleville.

I have so many memories that I could probably write a book. These are some of my good memories that I have of my younger years and I hope you all enjoy reliving them with me.

Memories from Dennis, Darrel, Delmar King

We grew up on the farm near Belleville that our parents bought from Grandpa Yoder in 1947. Grandpa and Grandma Yoder lived in Belleville just a couple miles from the farm so we often saw them at their house or ours. I can picture their green Chrysler coming in the farm lane when they came to visit us.

As a child, I remember going with Dad and Mother to see Grandma and Grandpa at their home on Walnut Street in Belleville. We visited in the living room, or we played in the front yard. There is a retaining wall at the edge of the yard along Walnut Street and extending along a lane to the farm behind their house. The wall seemed high, dangerous and scary. There was also a row of large lilac bushes along the lane near their garage. I remember a few things mother told us of her experiences growing up there. Being a large family, each of the children had assigned jobs around the house. She remembered the fun they had on a family trip to Washington, DC. As a teenager, she, her sisters Lola and Pauline and several girls in the neighborhood enjoyed doing things together and called themselves "The Weiner Gang".

Grandpa's coal and feed business was just down the street and across Kishacoquillas Creek. There were storage sheds and scales for weighing loaded trucks and his office was next to the scales. I can remember going with Dad to get feed or coal. Grandpa would be sitting in a swivel chair at his roll-top desk. In the winter, the little office was nice and warm from the coal stove next to his desk.

Following Grandpa's death, a mobile home was purchased in State College and placed near our house on the farm for Grandma to live closer to us. A screened in front porch was built for the mobile home. She enjoyed sitting by the window or on her screened porch to watch us working around the farm. One of us remembers Grandma scolding him for not playing nice with his younger brother. Grandma had television before we had TV in our house. So we liked going to her trailer to watch television - especially *Lassie* on Sunday evenings. *Perry Mason* was one of her favorite shows.

48

With Grandma living next door, we had many opportunities to see our uncles and aunts and to play with our cousins when they came to visit her. We had so much fun, and we have good memories of those times together! (See cousin's memories below.)

Before moving to a nursing home, Grandma lived in our home for a while so mother could care for her in the guest bedroom upstairs. I remember that as a very busy time for Mother as she cared for Grandma in addition to her responsibilities as a homemaker on the farm and the mother of three boys.

Memories from Peggy A. (Yoder) Knepper
I loved going to the farm in the summer and playing with cousins. It was a wonderful time in my life. Aunt Arvilla and Uncle Trennis were so good to me. I loved the farm and them very much. I remember going to Grandpa and Grandma's place when I was young and played with the toys on the floor. Grandma rocked in the rocking chair and talked to me while I played on the floor. Grandpa lay on the daybed in the living room.

Memories from Jim King
My memory of Grandma Yoder in the house trailer on the farm under the big tree is the strong smell of coffee (is my compulsion for strong black Starbucks inspired by her?) and her jolly laugh. That is my take away from my young age ten impressions of her: that she was about the levity of life. Every year in the spring we would travel from Indiana to Belleville, PA for a week of cousins on the farm and the Yoder/King farm offered endless possibilities for boy romps and adventure. Up to the brook above the farm where the vista of the valley was bucolic and restive. Down to the haymow in the big barn where long stuffy clover bale tunnels made scratchy arms and claustrophobic anxiousness. Rope swings across the vastness

of the mow have physical thrill as the rope creaked against the massive beams above. Strong mellow cow smells permeated this space, creating endless sensory memories for me and my brothers. The breakfasts were legendary, platters of sunny side up eggs and bacon, toast and fresh jam.....what wasn't there to like about our annual sojourn to the Roots?

Memories from John King

My earliest memories of Grandpa and Grandma are from our visits to Belleville when Reuben was still living. He was lying on a bed in the living room. Grandma was always jolly and happy to see us. My memories are of her living in the mobile home at the farm and at the nursing home in Lewistown. At the farm, I would visit with her for a short time and was quickly outdoors on the farm playing with Delmar and other cousins. The farm brings back memories: the hill and on up the mountain, the farm smells, the milking parlor and a large, friendly dog. One time my dad was riding the horse when the saddle came loose and he started sliding off! I remember Aunt Arvilla's good cooking, especially bacon and eggs before we departed on our long journey back to Goshen, IN. And Uncle Trennis was so friendly and always interested in us!

Memories from Patsy (Yoder) Bishop

When I was six or seven years old my mother contracted polio. She and my sister Peggy went to stay with her parents in Stone Valley. Dad, my sister Mary Jane, and I went to live with Grandpa and Grandma Yoder until Mom got well.

I remember the large meals Grandma made. Grandpa was a big eater and Grandma was a great cook! Sausage, fried potatoes, and stewed tomatoes were my favorites. I remember Grandpa coming home for lunch and then taking a nap on the daybed. That is when Mary Jane and I would go upstairs to the bedroom and play with the toys we had brought from home. We also enjoyed playing with the marble roller, a series of

50

chutes that the marbles rolled down. The pantry was a favorite place to "check out", as the smells were great!

Memories from Dick Goss

Grandma Yoder's kitchen had a wood burning cook stove where she spent a lot of time cooking and baking. A wood box was to the left of the cook stove in the corner of the room. A round kitchen table was in the center of the room and there was a dry sink (maybe two) near the back door. The wood box was rectangular in shape, about four feet in length. I remember on several occasions sitting on the wood box next to the warm cook stove eating a homemade moon pie and smelling delicious food that was being prepared.

I don't remember many details about the living room, but I do remember that Grandma Yoder had a treadle sewing machine in the living room along with other furniture. Treadle sewing machines were very popular in the late 1800s and early to mid-1900s. They were like a small desk with the essential parts of the sewing machine on top and with a cast iron flat foot treadle near the floor. Power to run the sewing machine was provided by exerting a pumping action with one's feet on the foot treadle. When I was about eight years old I used to like to sit on the floor under the sewing machine and push on the foot treadle to make the cast iron wheel go around. Unfortunately, I would sometimes get my fingers pinched between the cast iron treadle as it went up and down and the wooden floor.

If I recall correctly, rooms in Grandma and Grandpa Yoder's house had very old light switches by today's standards. Instead of the flush-mounted light switches that we have today, light switches in their house were the old cylindrical surface mounted kind; the kind that were installed in homes about 1900. When a light switch was turned on or off, it made a very loud distinct snapping noise.

One door in the living room led to Grandma's pantry. I was in the pantry only once. It was a dark and very small room with shelves on at least one wall. Unlike food storage areas in homes today, I recall that Grandma's pantry only had food that she had canned in Mason jars. When I was in the pantry I asked what was in one set of Mason jars and was told the jars contained mincemeat for making mincemeat pies.

Another door in the living room led to the parlor. The parlor door was kept closed most times because, unlike many homes with parlors that were used as sitting rooms, Grandma kept her quilting frame in the parlor. Grandma made many quilts and I still remember quilts she had given to our family in the mid-1950s. Our house near Lewistown had a coal burning furnace and many nights in the winter our bedrooms would get cold after the coal fire had burned down. Grandma's quilts were put to very good use.

In the early 1950s Grandpa Yoder had a four door sedan. I believe it was a dark green Chrysler, New Yorker, and if my memory serves me correctly, the features I recall are similar to pictures I have seen of the 1946 Chrysler, New Yorker. I remember one trip in that Chrysler in the early 1950s when my father, Charlie Goss, was the driver and my mother Lola, Sister Bonnie, and Brother Randy and I and some other relative (can't recall who it was) took a road trip to Titusville, PA to visit Paul and Pauline King and their children. I believe we spent one or two nights at Paul and Pauline's house and had a great time, but we had an unusual mechanical problem on our way to Titusville. At some point in the trip, the Chrysler's horn started blowing every time our father made a left turn. In those days, there were no interstate highways, so a traveler had to pass through many small towns and had to make numerous left and right turns. After going through several small towns and having local people look at us rather disapprovingly when the horn blew, my father finally got out of the car, raised the hood, and disconnected the horn.

Our mother, Lola Goss, would often call her mother, Grandma Yoder, from our home near Lewistown. We lived about 15 miles away from Grandma Yoder, but in the early 1950s, that was a long distance telephone call, and a telephone operator had to be called to complete the call. I vividly recall Grandma's phone number. When our mother would give the operator the phone number she would ask for "Belleville 35W". In later years, no one has ever been able to explain that number to me, but I believe the "W" may have indicated Walnut Street.

Memories of Susanne Lucille King

This crazy quilt, awakened from hibernation after my mother died, had slept for perhaps a century in the old pine blanket chest. I had never seen it before, a glorious composition of feathered stitches and remnants of 19th century clothes worn by my ancestors. My great grandmother's sister,

A Patchwork of Memories

Elizabeth Byler Yoder, had humbly stitched her initials and the 1896 date in a quiet corner.

My mother gave me a blue and white basket quilt that my great grandmother created for her when she was two years old. Her grandmother, Sarah Byler Yoder, wrote a note to accompany the quilt:

> "For Paline Yoder Peaced and Presented
> by her Grandmother Yoder in 1922"

"Blood is thicker than water," was not a saying I knew when I was ten years old. What I did know was the joy of anticipating the hundred-mile trip to Big Valley, where most of our relatives lived-grandparents, aunts and uncles, and many cousins. We only visited them several times a year, packing up the station wagon with boys and  diapers and sandwiches to sustain us on the three-hour-long journey, punctuated by threats from our father to stop the car if the ruckus in the back seat didn't settle down.

We arrived in Belleville, Pennsylvania after a long three-hour trip that included a drive through the paper mill stench of Tyrone, and at least two bathroom stops for my younger brothers. At the end of our voyage, we staggered onto the front porch of Grandpa and Grandma Yoder's white clapboard Victorian house. My grandparents would be sitting in their worn rockers waiting for us. We would dutifully kiss Grandpa's whiskery face, and hug our grandma's small round body. Even with my eyes closed, I knew I was entering Grandma Yoder's house, with its funky, earthy coffee smell.

Without further ceremony, I'd head to the front parlor, shut the door, and breathe a deep sigh of anticipation. The parlor was always cool, both in winter and summer. I'd sit on the piano stool, and pick out notes and chords from hymnals, like "Jesu, Heart of my Desiring," or practice Chopsticks and the Black Hawk Waltz, which my mother had taught me.

54

Ancestor paintings hung in our grandparents' house, young, handsome and serious people. I don't remember seeing them then.

Solomon & Nancy (Kaukkman) Zook

After our mother died, we found a postcard from Grandma Yoder to a friend in our mother's belongings, a message from the past capturing the voice and likeness of our grandmother in her youth, before we knew her.

Mary is 4th from the left in the back row

Family Recipes
The August heat and bumper crop of cucumbers in my garden I will transform into bread and butter pickles from a recipe in the Mennonite Community Cookbook, quickly take me back to childhood. My mother's techniques for simple dishes that required no recipes were supplemented by instructions from this book: chicken potpie, beet pickles, cinnamon rolls, lemon meringue pie, shoofly pie, taffy and divinity candy, all created from recipes in this, our only cookbook.

I didn't see Grandma Yoder's cookbook until seven years ago, when our cousin Bonnie graciously made copies of it for everyone at the 2006 Yoder family reunion. In this slim booklet Grandma recorded some of her favorite recipes and home remedies. The first page, in her own handwriting, is a delight, and her editorial comments are encouraging:

All of the recipes are for desserts, and two of them were handed down from her mother and mother-in-law: "Grandma Zook's cake receipt," and "Grandma Yoder's drop cookies, with molasses or not."

In addition to recipes, the booklet contains folk remedies, with several preparations for "rheumatism," which makes me suspect this was a malady from which either she or Grandpa suffered.

"Take mullen leaves and make a tea, drink 3 or 4 times a day - a cure."

"Pokeberries or poke roots are a cure for it, rheumatism, an Indian cure, 12 to 15 berries at a time, 3 or 4 times a day."

I am dubious about this advice for achy joints: "Take one teaspoonful sulfur in each shoe and it will cure it."

Cardiovascular disease also has a remedy: "Garlic will cure hardening of the arteries and high blood pressure, eat the stuff."

Urinary problems are addressed: "Tea of pipsissema - make it into tea and drink for bedwetting."

"Bull nettle tea 3 times a day, if not cured, sassafras tea or chew bark."

"Give child cinnamon bark to eat if it has weak bladder and this will cure."

As a psychiatrist who knows about anxiety, I find her last cure touching: "Nervousness - drink strong catnip tea before going to bed. A sure cure also good for sleepless nights." I do have to wonder about the nighttime effect of this remedy on a weak bladder.

Memories of Titus King

I and my sons Justin and Andre fit into the category of 'coffee snobs'. Coffee is a requisite conversation topic when we get together. (As it often is with my five sibs, I might add.) We like it black, dark roast, with intense flavor and lots of aroma. Is it environmentally or genetically influenced? Mother Pauline and my father Paul liked their coffee, albeit often the instant or the freeze-dried variety. "Good to the last drop" I recall from the Maxwell House metal cans of coffee in the kitchen when I first recognized coffee as a commodity. Grandma Mary Zook Yoder's Belleville Walnut Street house in the morning had the smell of coffee, percolated on the stove top in a metal pot with a glass knob on the lid. (It was strong coffee as I recall looking at it; and now I am only able to drink a cup of java if it is a stout one.) She and my mother savored drinking coffee together from thick ceramic cups on thick saucers. When my nuclear family lived in Troutville, PA in the nineteen fifties, similar cups and saucers, sold with firing defects at rock bottom discount prices from an outlet at the pottery factory in Brockway became the to-go-for coffee cups for my parents.

The Reuben and Mary Zook Yoder house on Walnut Street in Belleville had some places of interest for me as a kid. The garage behind the house on the alley was a converted carriage house style as I recall, with an exterior of clapboard wooden siding and four-light window panes, there being bare, exposed wooden wall studs and a 'dirt' floor on the interior. While I seem to remember a loft or a second floor, I do recall enjoying snooping around, checking out the relatively few items in the garage. One item was a quart size glass jar, a canning jar, with a metal funnel screwed on top, with a little residual motor oil in the bottom of the jar. This ole-timey utilitarian vessel was green! A reusable quart motor oil container; just fill it up from a two gallon metal oil can or from the 55 gallon drum of oil sitting horizontally on saw horses at the service station.

The garage during the second war to end all wars housed the family car, unused for long periods of time I was told. War rationing limited the amount of gasoline available, and since rubber primarily went to support the war efforts in the European and Pacific theaters my grandparents, like many others, jacked up the car so the wheels were not in contact with the earthen floor in an effort to lengthen the life of the rubber tires and tubes. Yes this was still the era of pre-tubeless and pre-radial belted tires, and rubber compounds deteriorated more quickly and the rubber in tires was subject to cracking.

Grandparent Yoder's garage was on a tree lined gravel alley. A row of tall trees, along with a single-strand barbed wire fence, and the alley separated the garage and house from a pasture field to the south. The bovines grazing in the field fascinated me. They were a herd of Holstein Friesians, unlike our single family Guernsey cow back in Clearfield County. Black and white ruminants sweeping amply long tongues in an arc to grab the pasture grass, then ripping-biting the tuft and swallowing. It was fascinating to watch the bulge, the wad of grass, move from the animals head down their neck to the first of their four stomachs. And to watch it move back up to their mouth to be chewed and mixed with saliva and re-swallowed. Much later in life I learned the term regurgitation, and when I had my own cattle on a gentlemen's farm in Michigan I learned that cows have teeth on the lower jaw and toughened gums on the upper jaw, which confirmed the ripping sound of the grass

58

being foraged that I heard as a kid while visiting my grandparents.

The creek was called a 'crik' in the regional pronunciation which shaped my vocabulary, found humorous by the New Yorkers of my days of alternate service as a conscientious objector at Bellevue Hospital in the late 60s. The creek flowed under the bridge near my Grandparent Yoder's house on Walnut Street. Part of my fascination with nature I'm sure was influenced early on by watching the gently flowing water of this small stream. And the ubiquitous meadow mint tea growing along the banks. And the cloven hoof prints in the mud of the creek bank where dairy cows had stood to drink in long, slow drafts of cool water. Mother's brother Merle had joined the military services. That was a wonder to me since my Mennonite pastor father and my mother were pacifist to the core. I thought all Mennonites were pacifists, until that bubble burst with Mother talking about her brother doing a stint as an enlistee, mind you. Once at the end of a whirlwind Big Valley visit to our numerous relatives on both sides of the family, drifting off to sleep in the back seat of the car which made the 2 1/2 hour drive back to Troutville pass in a flash, I heard Mother talking to Dad about some of the difficulties of family conversations on controversial topics. Including war versus peace positions.

At a memorial service recently for a nonagenarian mother of a friend, a granddaughter spoke about Grandma Ida, and her words reminded me of some of the things Grandmother Mary was want to say as well. And my mother as well. "Aye yi" (aye yai yai) was used when she wanted to convey that she didn't want to believe what she had just heard. Or an elongated "Oh my." Or "mercy me." And I remember the dental click, the tongue moving off the roof of the mouth in a "tsk, tsk" sound. Mother's sister Arvilla probably got her abbreviated "goodness" from one of her parent's "goodness me."

59

Mother Pauline's family were members of Maple Grove Mennonite Church. When we went there on a Sunday morning most family members sat together. Father Paul's family mostly went to Locust Grove Church. There men and boys all sat on the west side of the church and women and girls sat on the east side of the building. I don't ever remember Grandpa Reuben going to church with the rest of us. (I was young when he died so I have few memories of him in general.) Grandma Mary went until her health was compromised. I wish I could remember whether Grandma was a strong singer. Mother's strong alto was nurtured somehow. Maple Grove impressed me because it had a long tradition of eight part women's double octets. Yes, we're talking women singing two soprano, two alto, two women's tenor, and two women's baritone/bass parts. In the summer the unconditioned air of the church was sometimes stifling hot, even with the tall double-hung windows open. Grandma carried a paper hand fan, the hourglass shape style, and gave it a good workout to stay comfortable during the long sermons. The wooden, unpadded pews were hard as I recall. Grandma's Sunday clothes were newer models of what she wore during the week. Her summer clothing was a filmy, traditional, shirtwaist dress, amply tailored to accommodate her ample frame. Mother Pauline talked about nylon fabric becoming available during the 1930s and competing with cotton, then becoming scarce during the Second World War years of the 1940s.

Generation 8

8a. Alta Z. Yoder[8] YR25111441 (Reuben[7], Moses P[6], John H[5], Yost[4], Bishop John[3], John (Hans[2]), Christian[1])

Alta was born on Jan 18, 1912. She lived only two days and passed on Jan 20, 1912.

8b. Elton "Hicks" Saul Yoder[8] YR25111442 (Reuben[7], Moses P[6], John H[5], Yost[4], Bishop John[3], John (Hans[2]), Christian[1])

Elton & Ron Yoder

Elton was born on March 12, 1914 and died on Jan 19, 1972 in the state hospital in Harrisburg, PA. He is interred at Locust Grove Cemetery in Belleville, PA. On Aug 11, 1934 he married Verdie Irene Pearson. Verdie was born July 25, 1913 and passed on June 22, 2009 in Blairsville, GA. She is interred at the Lind Memorial cemetery in Lewistown, PA. Elton worked for his father in the coal yard until he was hospitalized in 1953. Elton and Verdie had three children.

> 9a. Donna Mae Yoder[9] YR251114421
> 9b. Phyllis Kay Yoder[9] YR251114422
> 9c. Ronald Fay Yoder[9] YR251114423

8c. Elmer David Yoder[8], YR25111443 (Reuben[7], Moses P[6], John H[5], Yost[4], Bishop John[3], John (Hans[2]), Christian[1])

Elmer was born on May 14, 1915 and died October 27, 1993. He is interred at Mooresville Cemetery, Huntingdon Co., PA. Elmer was married to Winifred "Sue" Belle Wilson. Sue was born May 7, 1920, and died Sept 25, 2007. Elmer and Sue had five daughters.

> 9d. Patricia Louise Yoder[9] YR251114431

9e. Mary Jane Yoder[9] YR251114432
9f. Peggy A. Yoder[9] YR251114433
9g. Susan Lee Yoder[9] YR251114434
9h. Deborah Jean Yoder[9] YR251114435

8d. Arvilla Mae Yoder[8] YR25111444 (Reuben[7], Moses P[6], John H[5], Yost[4], Bishop John[3], John (Hans[2]), Christian[1])

Arvilla was born on March 10, 1917 and passed on July 17, 2011. She is interred at Locust Grove Cemetery, Belleville, PA. On April 5, 1942 she was married to Trennis Samuel King. Trennis was born on April 8, 1917 and died on April 16, 2002. He is also interred at Locust Grove Cemetery, Belleville, PA.

Arvilla Mae Yoder

Trennis and Arvilla were born and grew up in the Kishacoquillas Valley of Mifflin County, PA; Trennis in Allensville and Arvilla in Belleville. Trennis was the oldest of three children and Arvilla the fourth of eight children. They met at Literary Society meetings for young people in Big Valley and were married April 5, 1942. They lived and farmed near White Hall and near Milroy until 1947 when they bought the farm east of Belleville from Arvilla's father, Reuben. They were the third generation of Yoders to own the farm, and the current owner, Brent King, is of the fifth generation. There they farmed and raised their three sons. In 1976 their youngest son Delmar took over the farm and they moved from the farmhouse to a house they built on the farm. Trennis then sold Funk seeds and Agri-King agricultural feed supplements. They moved to a cottage in the Valley View Retirement Community in 1996.

Trennis and Arvilla were both active members of Maple Grove Mennonite Church where Arvilla attended her entire life. They enjoyed serving as Sunday School teachers and on numerous committees and boards at Maple Grove and in the Allegheny Conference of Mennonite churches.

They were also involved at Belleville Mennonite School where Trennis served on the board for many years, eleven years as president. In the 1960's meetings were held and plans made for a nursing home in Belleville. Consequently, Valley View Haven opened in 1968. Trennis served on that board for twenty years, sixteen as chairman. Trennis and Arvilla lived the last years of their lives at Valley View. In the early 1980's they were among a group of people who met to discuss their interest in preserving the heritage of the Mennonites and Amish in Mifflin County. As a result, The Mifflin County Mennonite Historical Society was established in 1985 and the Mennonite Heritage Center opened in 1989. Trennis served as Board President from 1985-1992.

Throughout their lives they demonstrated their faith, their commitment to family and their desire to serve others. Trennis and Arvilla had three sons.

9i. Dennis Samuel King[9]
9j. Darrel Jay King[9]
9k. Delmar Ray King[9]

8e. Pauline Clare Yoder[8] YR25111445 (Reuben[7], Moses P[6], John H[5], Yost[4], Bishop John[3], John (Hans[2]), Christian[1]

Pauline was born on Nov 5, 1920 and passed on March 10, 2006. She was married to Paul Leonard King on April 1, 1944. Paul was born on April 11, 1920 and died on June 3, 1970.

Pauline Clair Yoder

Pauline graduated from Lancaster Business College and worked at Big Valley Pennsylvania Bank. Pauline and Paul moved to Goshen, Indiana in 1959 where she was office manager of a medical practice for 17 years. She was also a medical secretary for the nursing department of Goshen College and a transcriptionist in the Goshen College Administration Building.

Pauline served two-and-a-half years in the 1980s with Mennonite Central Committee at Hospital Albert Schweitzer in Haiti. She was a member of College Mennonite Church of Goshen and a member of Phalo Club.

Paul was an ordained minister. He and Pauline are interred at The Elkhart Prairie Cemetery in Indiana. They had six children.
    9l. Susanne Lucille King[9]
    9m. Titus Paul King[9]
    9n. Daniel Jacob King[9]
    9o. James Reuben King[9]
    9p. John Robert King[9]
    9q. David Philip King[9]

8f. Lola Lorraine Yoder[8] YR25111446 (Reuben[7], Moses P[6], John H[5], Yost[4], Bishop John[3], John (Hans[2]), Christian[1])

Lola was born on July 8, 1925. She graduated from Belleville High School in 1943.

Charlie Goss was a Lewistown native who had enlisted in the U.S. Army in March 1943, and was home on leave in 1944.

Lola Lorraine Yoder

While spending the day at "Kish" Park, a small local amusement park near Lewistown PA, Lola and Charlie met.

In December 1944, Charlie's Army division was transferred to Europe to participate in the war effort. Charlie was a truck driver for a field artillery battalion. While in Europe, he was stationed in France and Austria. Charlie returned to the U.S. and civilian life in April 1946.

In June 1946, Charlie and Lola married. In the early years of their marriage, Charlie worked at the American Viscose plant in Lewistown, a textile plant that made rayon products. Later, he was a truck driver. Charlie had a heart attack and died in 1965 at the age of 41.

Lola was a housewife and mother to their three children, Dick, Bonnie, and Randy. In 1964, Lola started working at the Lewistown Hospital. In the early 1970s, she completed Licensed Practical Nurse training and then moved to Mechanicsburg, PA where she worked at Holy Spirit Hospital. In 1985 she retired and moved back to her home in Lewistown where she lived until her death on April 12,

1990 at the age of 64. Lola is buried at Mt. Rock Cemetery, Mifflin Co., PA.

    9r. Richard Goss[9]
    9s. Bonita (Bonnie) Lorraine Goss[9]
    9t. Charles Randall Goss[9]

8g. Merle "Mose" Roy Yoder[8] YR25111447 (Reuben[7], Moses P[6], John H[5], Yost[4], Bishop John[3], John (Hans[2]), Christian[1])

Mose was born Oct 2, 1926 and died Feb 14, 2006. He served in the U.S. Army during WWII and was awarded the American Theatre Service Ribbon and the World War II Victory Medal. Mose worked most of his life at The New Holland Machine Company, retiring in 1989. He worked in the Press & Shear Department and in the Machine Shop.

Merle R. Yoder

Mose's first marriage to Arlene Bernice Crownover in 1948, produced one child. Arlene was born on October 5, 1932.
    9u. Rhonda M. Yoder[9] YR251114471

Mose met Elizabeth "Betty" J. Bloss at the Sunset Diner in Huntington, PA and married her on Aug 30, 1969. Betty was born Oct. 29, 1924. There were no children.

8h. Lucille "Lucy" Marian Yoder[8] YR25111448 (Reuben[7], Moses P[6], John H[5], Yost[4], Bishop John[3], John (Hans[2]), Christian[1])

Lucy was born in Belleville, PA on Oct 27, 1930 and died on Aug 4, 2012. She graduated from Belleville High School, in the class of 1948 and attended Goshen College for 2 years. After further training at Philadelphia General Hospital,

Lucy became a certified Laboratory Technician. She was employed at Grand View Hospital during the 1950's and later worked for many years in the family business.

Lucy served as chairwoman of the Goshen College Alumni Board and was also a member of Blooming Glen Mennonite Church where she served for 18 years as one of the first women

Lucille Marian Yoder

elders. She was also a Sunday school teacher, youth sponsor and church administrator. Lucy served in several leadership roles in the Franconia Mennonite Conference.

Lucy was married on July 7, 1951 to Robert Schueck Gotwals, a marriage that was celebrated for 61 years. Bob was born on July 12, 1929. This union produced three children.

9v. Susan Marie Gotwals[9]

9w. Robert Brent Gotwals[9]

9x. Christopher Kent Gotwals[9]

Generation 9

Some of the Yoder "Cousins" at the 2010 Reunion
standing in front of Reuben and Mary Yoder's home on
Walnut St. in Belleville

9a. Donna Mae Yoder[9] YR251114421 (Elton[8], Reuben[7], Moses P[6], John H[5], Yost[4], Bishop John[3], John (Hans[2]), Christian[1])

Donna was born on April 29, 1936. Donna has been married twice. Marriage 1 was to Lloyd Colyer. This marriage produced three children.
    10a. Timothy Lloyd Colyer[10]
    10b. Donna Diane Colyer[10]
    10c. Larry Scott Colyer[10]
Donna's second marriage was to Gene Wesley Henninger on August 11, 1965. Gene was born Jan 24, 1938. This union produced one son.
    10d. Robert Bryan Henninger[10]

9b. Phyllis Kay Yoder[9] YR251114422 (Elton[8], Reuben[7], Moses P[6], John H[5], Yost[4], Bishop John[3], John (Hans[2]), Christian[1])

Phyllis was born on April 1, 1938 and died at the age of 5 of Brights disease on Dec 12, 1943.

9c. Ronald "Ron" Fay Yoder[9] YR251114423 (Elton[8], Reuben[7], Moses P[6], John H[5], Yost[4], Bishop John[3], John (Hans[2]), Christian[1])

Ron was born on April 2, 1943 in Belleville. On March 24, 1964 he married Gloria Diane Swartzell, born Mar 16, 1944. They produced two sons who will carry on the Yoder name.
> 10e. Gregory Lynn Yoder[10] YR 2511144231
> 10f. Douglas Wade Yoder[10] YR2511144232

9d. Patricia Louise Yoder[9] YR251114431 (Elmer[8], Reuben[7], Moses P[6], John H[5], Yost[4], Bishop John[3], John (Hans[2]), Christian[1])

Pat was born on July 10, 1940 and married Eugene Samuel Bishop on Jan 31, 1960 and together they produced two children.
> 10g. Elizabeth Ann Bishop[10]
> 10h. Angela Joy Bishop[10]

9e. Mary Jane Yoder[9] YR251114432 (Elmer[8], Reuben[7], Moses P[6], John H[5], Yost[4], Bishop John[3], John (Hans[2]), Christian[1])

Mary Jane was born on Oct 2, 1941 and died April 28, 2004. She was married to Russell Simpson.

9f. Peggy A. Yoder[9] YR251114433 (Elmer[8], Reuben[7], Moses P[6], John H[5], Yost[4], Bishop John[3], John (Hans[2]), Christian[1])

Peggy was born on April 25, 1944 and was married to William L. Knepper on Dec 4, 1960. William was born on July 1, 1936. This union produced one child.
> 10i. Pamela S. Knepper[10]

9g. Susan Lee Yoder[9] YR251114434 (Elmer[8], Reuben[7], Moses P[6], John H[5], Yost[4], Bishop John[3], John (Hans[2]), Christian[1])

Susan was born on Jan 25, 1948 and married Vernon Daubert on Oct 15, 1966. Vernon was born Dec 16, 1945. They have three children.

    10j. Tracy L. Daubert[10]
    10k. Joseph V. Daubert[10]
    10l. Brian Lee Daubert[10]

9h. Deborah "Debbie" Jean Yoder[9] YR251114435 (Elmer[8], Reuben[7], Moses P[6], John H[5], Yost[4], Bishop John[3], John (Hans[2]), Christian[1])

Debbie was born on Dec 29, 1951. She was married twice, first to Alan Hartley and second to Jerry Gillet. The first union produced one child.

    10m. Michelle Renee Hartley[10]

9i. Dennis Samuel King[9] (Arvilla [8], Reuben[7], Moses P[6], John H[5], Yost[4], Bishop John[3], John (Hans[2]), Christian[1])

Dennis was born on Feb 7, 1947. On Sept 11, 1970 he married Judy L. Harding. Judy was born on Mar 1, 1946. This union produced two children.

    10n. Bradley Dennis King[10]
    10o. Katherine Harding King[10]

9j. Darrel Jay King[9] (Arvilla[8], Reuben[7], Moses P[6], John H[5], Yost[4], Bishop John[3], John (Hans[2]), Christian[1])

Darrel was born on Oct 3, 1948. On Nov 7, 1970 he married Sara Jane Yoder. Sara Jane was born on Dec 2, 1949. This marriage produced three sons.

    10p. Scott Michael King[10]
    10q. Anthony J. King[10]
    10r. Mathew Brent King[10]

9k. Delmar Ray King[9] (Arvilla[8], Reuben[7], Moses P[6], John H[5], Yost[4], Bishop John[3], John (Hans[2]), Christian[1])

Delmar was born on June 29, 1952. On June 30, 1973 he was married to Sandra Mae Glick. Sandra was born on May 9, 1954. Together they produced three children.
    10s. Crystal Lynn King[10]
    10t. Amy Jo King[10]
    10u. Brent Michael King[10]

9l. Susanne Lucille King[9] (Pauline[8], Reuben[7], Moses P[6], John H[5], Yost[4], Bishop John[3], John (Hans[2]), Christian[1])

Susanne was born on Jan 22, 1945. On March 9, 1981 she married Richard Marc Berlin. Richard was born on April 27, 1950. They have one daughter.
    10v. Rachel King Berlin[10]

9m. Titus Paul King[9] (Pauline[8], Reuben[7], Moses P[6], John H[5], Yost[4], Bishop John[3], John (Hans[2]), Christian[1])

Titus was born on May 30, 1946. Titus has been married twice. His first marriage was to Kathleen Louise Mast on April 19, 1969. Kathleen was born on Mar 20, 1947 and this union produced two children.
    10w. Justin Saul King[10]
    10x. Andre Christian King[10]

Titus' second marriage was to Joy Amelia Kroft-Kauffman on Sept 14, 2002. Joy was born on Sept 10, 1942. She has three children by a previous marriage.
    Heidi Marie Kauffman
    Karl Jon Kauffman
    Troy Galen Kauffman

9n. Daniel Jacob King[9] (Pauline[8], Reuben[7], Moses P[6], John H[5], Yost[4], Bishop John[3], John (Hans[2]), Christian[1])

Daniel was born on June 17, 1949. On July 8, 1972 he was married to Gloria Ann Loucks. Gloria was born on Aug 23, 1952. Together they produced two children.
    10y. Carmine Sue King[10]
    10z. Nathan Daniel King[10]

9o. James Reuben King[9] (Pauline[8], Reuben[7], Moses P[6], John H[5], Yost[4], Bishop John[3], John (Hans[2]), Christian[1])

James was born Oct 4, 1952. He and John are twins. He remains single.

9p. John Robert King[9] (Pauline[8], Reuben[7], Moses P[6], John H[5], Yost[4], Bishop John[3], John (Hans[2]), Christian[1])

John, like his twin, James, was born on Oct 4, 1952. John married Kelli Evelyn Burkholder, born May 28, 1955 and they produced two children.
    10aa. Jacob Hans King[10]
    10ab. Suzanne Marissa King[10]

9q. David Philip King[9] (Pauline[8], Reuben[7], Moses P[6], John H[5], Yost[4], Bishop John[3], John (Hans[2]), Christian[1])

David was born Oct 1, 1957 in DuBois, PA. David was married twice with the second marriage to Patricia Leonor Michelsen producing one child. David and Patricia were married on June 9, 1996 in Richmond, VA. Patricia was born on July 6, 1952 in Bogotá, Columbia.
    10ac. Alejandro David King [10]

Patricia brought four children into the marriage.
>Tanya Carolina Lord
>Michele Carolina Lord
>Arthur Richard Lord
>Mathew Allen Whitley

9r. Richard Goss[9] (Lola[8], Reuben[7], Moses P[6], John H[5], Yost[4], Bishop John[3], John (Hans[2]), Christian[1])

Richard was born in 1947. He is married to Linda Black who was born in 1950. They were married in 1968 and have one son.
>10ad. Mark Goss[10]

9s. Bonita (Bonnie) Lorraine Goss[9] (Lola[8], Reuben[7], Moses P[6], John H[5], Yost[4], Bishop John[3], John (Hans[2]), Christian[1])

Bonita was born on April 3, 1948. On Dec 10, 1971 she was married to David Haigh Watson. David was born on Dec 3, 1944. They produced two children.
>10ae. Angela Loraine Watson[10]
>10af. Kari Elizabeth Watson[10]

9t. Charles Randall Goss[9] (Lola[8], Reuben[7], Moses P[6], John H[5], Yost[4], Bishop John[3], John (Hans[2]), Christian[1])

Charles was born on Jan 9, 1950 and was married twice. His first marriage to Donna L. Gearhart in 1973 produced one son.
>10ag. Michael Alan Goss[10]

On July 21, 1984 Charles married Laura Evelyn Brown. Laura was born Jan 17, 1960. This union produced two children.
>10ah. Nathan Tyler Goss[10]
>10ai. Rebecca Marie Goss[10]

9u. Rhonda M. Yoder[9] YR251114471 (Merle[8], Reuben[7], Moses P[6], John H[5], Yost[4], Bishop John[3], John (Hans[2]), Christian[1])

Rhonda was born Feb 21, 1949. She married Paul Letso and they produced two children.
    10aj. Paul Letso[10]
    10ak. Alissa Letso[10]

9v. Susan Marie Gotwals[9] (Lucille[8], Reuben[7], Moses P[6], John H[5], Yost[4], Bishop John[3], John (Hans[2]), Christian[1])

Susan was born on Jan 20, 1953. She was married twice, first to Joseph Anthony Rody on July 24, 1982. Joseph was born on Aug 17, 1955 and this union produced two children.
    10al. Mathew Gotwals Rody[10]
    10am. Sarah Gotwals Rody[10]

Susan's second marriage was to Timothy Lewman on Aug 11, 1996. Timothy was born Sept 5, 1952. Susan and Timothy have no children.

9w. Robert Brent Gotwals[9] (Lucille[8], Reuben[7], Moses P[6], John H[5], Yost[4], Bishop John[3], John (Hans[2]), Christian[1])

Robert was born on Dec 20, 1954. On July 22, 1978 he married Julia Detweiler. Julia was born on Sept 19, 1955. They have three children.
    10an. Erin Lynn Gotwals[10]
    10ao. Alison Kate Gotwals[10]
    10ap. Jessica Rae Gotwals[10]

9x. Christopher Kent Gotwals[9] (Lucille[8], Reuben[7], Moses P[6], John H[5], Yost[4], Bishop John[3], John (Hans[2]), Christian[1])

Christopher was born on Dec 11, 1965. On Dec 27, 1996 he married Kathleen Schlegel. Kathleen was born on Nov 4, 1962. This union produced two children.

10aq. Christopher Daniel Gotwals[10]

10ar. Kira Nicole Gotwals[10]

Generation 10

10a. Timothy Lloyd Colyer[10] (Donna[9], Elton[8], Reuben[7], Moses P[6], John H[5], Yost[4], Bishop John[3], John (Hans[2]), Christian[1])
b: 11/17/1952, d: 10/29/2000

10b. Donna Diane Colyer[10] (Donna[9], Elton[8], Reuben[7], Moses P[6], John H[5], Yost[4], Bishop John[3], John (Hans[2]), Christian[1])
b: 11/2/1955

Diane was married twice. Her marriage to Robert Dana Downard produced one child. Dana died in 2001.
    11a. Alicia Mae Downard[11]
Her second marriage to Bobbie Jo Talbot on 1/14/1994 produced no children.

10c. Larry Scott Colyer[10] (Donna[9], Elton[8], Reuben[7], Moses P[6], John H[5], Yost[4], Bishop John[3], John (Hans[2]), Christian[1])
b: 2/12/1957

Larry was married twice. His first marriage was to Pamela Snizer b: 1957. There were no children by his first marriage.

Larry married Patti Gentry on 9/15/1979. Patti was born 8/15/1961. This union produced two children.
    11b. Megan DeAnne Colyer[11]
    11c. Machaila Kyra Colyer[11]

10d. Robert Bryan Henninger[10] (Donna[9], Elton[8] Reuben[7], Moses P[6], John H[5], Yost[4], Bishop John[3], John (Hans[2]), Christian[1])
b: 7/30/1964

Robert married Kelly Brown Speckman on 5/3/1991. Kelly was born on 11/2/1969. They produced two daughters.

> 11d. Katie Maelyn Henninger[11]
> 11e. Rachel Brown Henninger[11]

10e. Gregory Lynn Yoder[10] YR 2511144231 (Ronald[9], Elton[8], Reuben[7], Moses P[6], John H[5], Yost[4], Bishop John[3], John (Hans[2]), Christian[1]) b: 9/17/1964

Gregory was married twice. The first marriage to Christine Pellman produced no children.

Greg's second marriage on 10/25/1992 to Ann Frances Lacerte, born on 11/8/1956, produced two children.

> 11f. Greer Elizabeth Yoder[11] YR 25111442311
> 11g. Bryce Gregory Yoder[11] YR 25111442312

10f. Douglas Wade Yoder[10] YR2511144232 (Ronald[9], Elton[8], Reuben[7], Moses P[6], John H[5], Yost[4], Bishop John[3], John (Hans[2]), Christian[1]) b: 2/29/1968

Douglas married Crystal Lynn Laub on 5/15/1993. Crystal was born on 3/19/1968. This union produced three sons.

> 11h. Addison James Yoder[11] YR25111442321
> 11i. Graydon Ellis Yoder[11]YR25111442322
> 11j. Zane Douglas Yoder[11]YR25111442323

10g. Elizabeth Ann Bishop[10] (Patricia[9], Elmer[8], Reuben[7], Moses P[6], John H[5], Yost[4], Bishop John[3], John (Hans[2]), Christian[1]) b: 2/1/1962

Elizabeth married Steven J. Auker on 6/4/1983. Steven was born on 3/29/1960. Together they produced three children.

11k. Kyle Steven Auker[11]
11l. Kayla Elizabeth Auker[11]
11m. Kelsey Elizabeth Auker[11]

10h. Angela Joy Bishop[10] (Patricia[9], Elmer[8], Reuben[7], Moses P[6], John H[5], Yost[4], Bishop John[3], John (Hans[2]), Christian[1])
b: 9/20/1965

Angela married Dennis R. Patterson on September 15, 1990. Dennis was born 1/13/1963. This union produced two children.
11n. Ashley Sue Patterson[11]
11o. Dylan James Patterson[11]

10i. Pamela S. Knepper[10] (Peggy[9], Elmer[8], Reuben[7], Moses P[6], John H[5], Yost[4], Bishop John[3], John (Hans[2]), Christian[1])
b: 5/10/1961

Pamela married Raymond Mark Drall on 5/30/1981. Raymond was born on 4/1/1957. This union produced four children.
11p. Nathon M. Drall[11]
11q. Jessica L. Drall[11]
11r. Nicholas W. Drall[11]
11s. Michael R. Drall[11]

10j. Tracy L. Daubert[10] (Susan[9], Elmer[8], Reuben[7], Moses P[6], John H[5], Yost[4], Bishop John[3], John (Hans[2]), Christian[1])
b: 1/19/1968

Tracy married Jerry Miller on 5/17/1996 and together they produced three children. Jerry Miller was born on 5/19/1966.
11t. Stephanie S. Miller[11]
11u. MacKenzie Miller[11]
11v. Kylie Jo Miller[11]

10k. Joseph V. Daubert[10] (Susan[9], Elmer[8], Reuben[7], Moses P[6], John H[5], Yost[4], Bishop John[3], John (Hans[2]), Christian[1]) b: 10/19/1970

Joseph first married Kathy (name unknown). This marriage produced one child.
11w. Amanda M. Daubert[11]

His second marriage was to Laura Lockett. They were married on 2/22/2013 and produced one child.
11x. Adan J. Daubert[11]

10l. Brian Lee Daubert[10] (Susan[9], Elmer[8], Reuben[7], Moses P[6], John H[5], Yost[4], Bishop John[3], John (Hans[2]), Christian[1]) b: 1/24/1973

10m. Michelle Renee Hartley[10] (Deborah[9], Elmer[8], Reuben[7], Moses P[6], John H[5], Yost[4], Bishop John[3], John (Hans[2]), Christian[1]) b: June 1971, d: 1976

10n. Bradley Dennis King[10] (Dennis[9], Arvilla[8,] Reuben[7], Moses P[6], John H[5], Yost[4], Bishop John[3], John (Hans[2]), Christian[1]) b: 1/7/1976

Bradley married Jill Fanders on 5/30/1998. Jill was born on 4/28/1976. They have one child.
11y. Isaac Bradley King[11]

10o. Katherine Harding King[10] (Dennis[9], Arvilla[8,] Reuben[7], Moses P[6], John H[5], Yost[4], Bishop John[3], John (Hans[2]), Christian[1]) b: 5/27/1979

Katherine married Gregory Mitchell on 6/1/2003. Gregory was born on 2/28/1980. This union produced two children.

> 11z. Eleanor Claire Mitchell[11]
> 11aa. Ian Gregory Mitchell[11]

10p. Scott Michael King[10] (Darrel[9], Arvilla[8], Reuben[7], Moses P[6], John H[5], Yost[4], Bishop John[3], John (Hans[2]), Christian[1])
b: 4/3/1971

Scott married Esther Ruth Cole on 12/15/2007. They have three children. Esther was born on 3/23/1984.

> 11ab. Coleson King[11]
> 11ac. Truett King[11]
> 11ad. Lachlan King[11]

10q. Anthony J. King[10] (Darrel[9], Arvilla[8], Reuben[7], Moses P[6], John H[5], Yost[4], Bishop John[3], John (Hans[2]), Christian[1])
b: 7/16/1973

Anthony married Cynthia M. Madden on 10/17/1992. They have produced five children.

> 11ae. Zachary Garret King[11]
> 11af. Kayla King[11]
> 11ag. Hayden King[11]
> 11ah. Samantha King[11]
> 11ai. Silas King[11]

10r. Mathew Brent King[10] (Darrel[9], Arvilla[8], Reuben[7], Moses P[6], John H[5], Yost[4], Bishop John[3], John (Hans[2]), Christian[1])
b: 9/29/1977

10s. Crystal Lynn King[10] (Delmar[9], Arvilla[8], Reuben[7], Moses P[6], John H[5], Yost[4], Bishop John[3], John (Hans[2]), Christian[1])
b: 6/29/1975

Crystal has been married twice. Her first marriage to Andrew Michael Westover in June 1998 produced one child.

      11aj. Drew Michael Westover[11]

Her second marriage to Harold Benfer on 7/7/2007 produced two children. Harold was born on 11/19/1980.

      11ak. Hunter Lee Benfer[11]
      11al. Chase Benfer[11]

10t. Amy Jo King[10] (Delmar[9], Arvilla[8,] Reuben[7], Moses P[6], John H[5], Yost[4], Bishop John[3], John (Hans[2]), Christian[1])
b: 6/14/1977

Amy Jo was married twice. Her first marriage to Michael A.S. Hood on 5/31/1996 produced one child.

      11am. Megan Nichole King[11]

Amy Jo's second marriage was to Daniel Robert Aumiller on 8/4/2001. Daniel was born on 10/11/1974.

10u. Brent Michael King[10] (Delmar[9], Arvilla[8,] Reuben[7], Moses P[6], John H[5], Yost[4], Bishop John[3], John (Hans[2]), Christian[1])
b: 11/22/1980

Brent married Rachel Sellers on 7/17/2004. Rachel was born on 4/17/1980. They have two children.

      11an. Hanna Marie King[11]
      11ao. Brooke Elizabeth King[11]

A point of interest: Rachel once lived in the same house on Coffee Run as our second generation, John "Hans" Yoder YR25.

10v. Rachel King Berlin[10] (Susanne[9], Pauline[8], Reuben[7], Moses P[6], John H[5], Yost[4], Bishop John[3], John (Hans[2]), Christian[1]) b: 2/20/1983

Rachel married Robert Nelson Gonzalez.

10w. Justin Saul King[10] (Titus[9], Pauline[8], Reuben[7], Moses P[6], John H[5], Yost[4], Bishop John[3], John (Hans[2]), Christian[1]) b: 11/30/1974

Justin married Sherry Cong Xin Fang on 5/23/2009. Sherry was born on 2/8/1980. They have one child.
    11ap. Timothy Yi King[11]

10x. Andre Christian King[10] (Titus[9], Pauline[8], Reuben[7], Moses P[6], John H[5], Yost[4], Bishop John[3], John (Hans[2]), Christian[1]) b: 7/2/1976

Andre married Sarah Anne Reis on 10/6/2001. Sarah Anne was born on 8/15/1976. They were divorced in Oct 2011 without child.

10y. Carmine Sue King[10] (Daniel[9], Pauline[8], Reuben[7], Moses P[6], John H[5], Yost[4], Bishop John[3], John (Hans[2]), Christian[1]) b: 9/22/1973

Carmine was married on 2/28/1998 to Thomas Shane Snyder. Thomas was born on 9/13/1967. This union produced two children.
    11aq. Hayden Thomas Snyder[11]
    11ar. Hunter Daniel Snyder[11]

10z. Nathan Daniel King[10] (Daniel[9], Pauline[8], Reuben[7], Moses P[6], John H[5], Yost[4], Bishop John[3], John (Hans[2]), Christian[1]) b: 4/12/1976

Nathan was married on 3/17/2001 to Angela Summer Mishler. Angela was born on 5/9/1979. They have three children.

> 11as. Brady Nathaniel King^{11}
> 11at. Austin Daniel King^{11}
> 11au. Ava Summer King^{11}

10aa. Jacob Hans King^{10} (John^9, Pauline^8, Reuben^7, Moses P^6, John H^5, Yost^4, Bishop John^3, John (Hans^2), Christian^1) b: 2/9/1986

Jacob married Carrie Joy Keagy in May 2010. Carrie was born on 12/24/1984. This union produced one child.

> 11av. Rivers C. King^{11}

10ab. Suzanne Marissa King^{10} (John^9, Pauline^8, Reuben^7, Moses P^6, John H^5, Yost^4, Bishop John^3, John (Hans^2), Christian^1) b: 3/17/1991

10ac Alejandro David King ^{10}(David^9, Pauline^8, Reuben^7, Moses P^6, John H^5, Yost^4, Bishop John^3, John (Hans^2), Christian^1) b: 6/17/1997

10ad. Mark Goss^{10} (Richard^9, Lola^8, Reuben^7, Moses P^6, John H^5, Yost^4, Bishop John^3, John (Hans^2), Christian^1) b: 1978

Mark was married to Jennifer Ludwig in 2006. Jennifer was born 1n 1979. This union produced two children.

> 11aw. Reese Goss^{11}
> 11ax. Delaney Goss^{11}

10ae. Angela Loraine Watson^{10} (Bonita^9, Lola^8, Reuben^7, Moses P^6, John H^5, Yost^4, Bishop John^3, John (Hans^2), Christian^1) b: 12/3/1972

10af. Kari Elizabeth Watson[10] (Bonita[9], Lola[8], Reuben[7], Moses P[6], John H[5], Yost[4], Bishop John[3], John (Hans[2]), Christian[1]) b: 12/10/1980

10ag. Michael Alan Goss[10] (Charles[9], Lola[8,] Reuben[7], Moses P[6], John H[5], Yost[4], Bishop John[3], John (Hans[2]), Christian[1]) b: 11/4/1979

Michael married Jessica Copenhaver 5/22/2010. Jessica was born on 8/28/1981.

10ah. Nathan Tyler Goss[10] (Charles[9], Lola[8], Reuben[7], Moses P[6], John H[5], Yost[4], Bishop John[3], John (Hans[2]), Christian[1]) b: 1/22/1986

10ai. Rebecca Marie Goss[10] (Charles[9], Lola[8], Reuben[7], Moses P[6], John H.[5], Yost[4], Bishop John[3], John (Hans[2]), Christian[1]) b: 5/9/1988

10aj. Paul Letso[10] (Rhonda[9], Merle[8], Reuben[7], Moses P[6], John H[5], Yost[4], Bishop John[3], John (Hans[2]), Christian[1])

10ak. Alissa Letso[10] (Rhonda[9], Merle[8], Reuben[7], Moses P[6], John H[5], Yost[4], Bishop John[3], John (Hans[2]), Christian[1])

10al. Mathew Gotwals Rody[10] (Susan[9], Lucille[8], Reuben[7], Moses P[6], John H[5], Yost[4], Bishop John[3], John (Hans[2]), Christian[1]) b: 5/13/1986

Mathew married Brooke Wassmann. Brooke was born on 2/24/1980.

10am. Sarah Gotwals Rody[10] (Susan[9], Lucille[8], Reuben[7], Moses P[6], John H[5], Yost[4], Bishop John[3], John (Hans[2]), Christian[1]) b: 10/14/1989

10an. Erin Lynn Gotwals[10] (Robert[9], Lucille[8], Reuben[7], Moses P[6], John H[5], Yost[4], Bishop John[3], John (Hans[2]), Christian[1]) b: 11/22/1984

10ao. Alison Kate Gotwals[10] (Robert[9], Lucille[8], Reuben[7], Moses P[6], John H[5], Yost[4], Bishop John[3], John (Hans[2]), Christian[1]) b: 9/11/1987

Allison married Andrew Brubaker on 7/31/2010. Andrew was born on 10/4/1987.

10ap. Jessica Rae Gotwals[10] (Robert[9], Lucille[8], Reuben[7], Moses P[6], John H[5], Yost[4], Bishop John[3], John (Hans[2]), Christian[1]) b: 1/28/1991

10aq. Christopher Daniel Gotwals[10] (Christopher[9], Lucille[8], Reuben[7], Moses P[6], John H[5], Yost[4], Bishop John[3], John (Hans[2]), Christian[1]) b: 11/4/1999

10ar. Kira Nicole Gotwals[10] (Christopher[9], Lucille Yoder[8], Reuben[7], Moses P[6], John H[5], Yost[4], Bishop John[3], John (Hans[2]), Christian[1]) b: 8/19/2002

Generation 11

11a. Alicia Mae Downard[11] (Diane[10], Donna[9], Elton[8] Reuben[7], Moses P[6], John H[5], Yost[4], Bishop John[3], John (Hans[2]), Christian[1]) b: 11/29/1978

11b. Megan DeAnne Colyer[11] (Larry[10], Donna[9] Elton[8] Reuben[7], Moses P[6], John H[5], Yost[4], Bishop John[3], John (Hans[2]), Christian[1]) b: 12/8/1987

11c. Machaila Kyra Colyer [11](Larry[10], Donna[9], Elton[8], Reuben[7], Moses P[6], John H[5], Yost[4], Bishop John[3], John (Hans[2]), Christian[1]) b: 5/25/1998

11d. Katie Maelyn Henninger[11] (Robert[10], Donna[9] Elton[8], Reuben[7], Moses P[6], John H[5], Yost[4], Bishop John[3], John (Hans[2]), Christian[1]) b: 1/10/1997

11e. Rachel Brown Henninger[11] (Robert[10], Donna[9], Elton[8] Reuben[7], Moses P[6], John H[5], Yost[4], Bishop John[3], John (Hans[2]), Christian[1]) b: 9/19/1999

11f. Greer Elizabeth Yoder[11] YR25111442311 (Gregory[10], Ronald[9], Elton[8], Reuben[7], Moses P[6], John H[5], Yost[4], Bishop John[3], John (Hans[2]), Christian[1]) b: 4/6/1995

11g. Bryce Gregory Yoder[11] YR 25111442312 (Gregory[10], Ronald[9], Elton[8], Reuben[7], Moses P[6], John H[5], Yost[4], Bishop John[3], John (Hans[2]), Christian[1]) b: 12/2/1998

11h. Addison James Yoder[11] YR25111442321 (Douglas[10], Ronald[9], Elton[8], Reuben[7], Moses P[6], John H[5], Yost[4], Bishop John[3], John (Hans[2]), Christian[1]) b: 8/25/1994

11i. Graydon Ellis Yoder[11]YR25111442322 (Douglas[10], Ronald[9], Elton[8] Reuben[7], Moses P[6], John H[5], Yost[4], Bishop John[3], John (Hans[2]), Christian[1]) b: 1/1/1996

11j. Zane Douglas Yoder[11]YR25111442323 (Douglas[10], Ronald[9], Elton[8] Reuben[7], Moses P[6], John H[5], Yost[4], Bishop John[3], John (Hans[2]), Christian[1]) b: 12/19/1998

11k. Kyle Steven Auker[11] (Elizabeth[10], Patricia[9], Elmer[8], Reuben[7], Moses P[6], John H[5], Yost[4], Bishop John[3], John (Hans[2]), Christian[1]) b: 12/5/1986

Kyle has one child.
12a. Cooper James Auker[12]

11l. Kayla Elizabeth Auker[11] (Elizabeth[10], Patricia[9], Elmer[8], Reuben[7], Moses P[6], John H[5], Yost[4], Bishop John[3], John (Hans[2]), Christian[1]) b: 3/9/1992, d: 3/9/1992

11m. Kelsey Elizabeth Auker[11] (Elizabeth[10], Patricia[9], Elmer[8], Reuben[7], Moses P[6], John H[5], Yost[4], Bishop John[3], John (Hans[2]), Christian[1]) b: 6/7/1993

11n. Ashley Sue Patterson[11] (Angela[10], Patricia[9], Elmer[8], Reuben[7], Moses P[6], John H[5], Yost[4], Bishop John[3], John (Hans[2]), Christian[1]) b: 10/15/1985

Ashley has one child.
12b. Cohen J. Patterson[12]

11o. Dylan James Patterson[11] (Angela[10], Patricia[9], Elmer[8], Reuben[7], Moses P[6], John H[5], Yost[4], Bishop John[3], John (Hans[2]), Christian[1]) b: 7/9/1992

11p. Nathon M. Drall[11] (Pamela[10], Peggy[9], Elmer[8], Reuben[7], Moses P[6], John H[5], Yost[4], Bishop John[3], John (Hans[2]), Christian[1]) b: 7/12/1982

11q. Jessica L. Drall[11] (Pamela[10], Peggy[9], Elmer[8], Reuben[7], Moses P[6], John H[5], Yost[4], Bishop John[3], John (Hans[2]), Christian[1]) b: 8/16/1983

Jessica married John Zuch on 6/13/2009. John was born on 8/17/1984. They have three children.
12c. Sierra Zuch[12]
12d. Roary Zuch[12]
12e. Lincoln Michael Zuch[12]

11r. Nicholas W. Drall[11] (Pamela[10], Peggy[9], Elmer[8], Reuben[7], Moses P[6], John H[5], Yost[4], Bishop John[3], John (Hans[2]), Christian[1]) b: 4/21/1987

Nicholas married Anna Long on 7/21/2012. Anna was born on 5/16/1990.

11s. Michael R. Drall[11] (Pamela[10], Peggy[9], Elmer[8], Reuben[7], Moses P[6], John H[5], Yost[4], Bishop John[3], John (Hans[2]), Christian[1]) b: 8/30/1989

11t. Stephanie S. Miller[11] (Tracy[10], Susan[9], Elmer[8], Reuben[7], Moses P[6], John H[5], Yost[4], Bishop John[3], John (Hans[2]), Christian[1]) b: 11/7/1989

Stephanie married Sam Dye on 6/30/2012. They have one child.
12f. Jeffrey Edward Dye b: 9/2/2013

11u. MacKenzie Miller[11] (Tracy[10], Susan[9], Elmer[8], Reuben[7], Moses P[6], John H[5], Yost[4], Bishop John[3], John (Hans[2]), Christian[1]) b: 7/23/1998

11v. Kylie Jo Miller[11] (Tracy[10], Susan[9], Elmer[8], Reuben[7], Moses P[6], John H[5], Yost[4], Bishop John[3], John (Hans[2]), Christian[1]) b: 2/1/2001

11w. Amanda M. Daubert[11] (Joseph[10], Susan[9], Elmer[8], Reuben[7], Moses P[6], John H[5], Yost[4], Bishop John[3], John (Hans[2]), Christian[1]) b: 5/30/1997

11x. Adan J. Daubert[11] (Joseph[10], Susan[9], Elmer[8], Reuben[7], Moses P[6], John H[5], Yost[4], Bishop John[3], John (Hans[2]), Christian[1]) b: 12/7/2007

11y. Isaac Bradley King[11] (Bradley[10], Dennis[9], Arvilla[8], Reuben[7], Moses P[6], John H[5], Yost[4], Bishop John[3], John (Hans[2]), Christian[1]) b: 8/20/2004

11z. Eleanor Claire Mitchell[11] (Katherine[10], Dennis[9], Arvilla[8], Reuben[7], Moses P[6], John H[5], Yost[4], Bishop John[3], John (Hans[2]), Christian[1]) b: 1/9/2008

11aa. Ian Gregory Mitchell[11] (Katherine[10], Dennis[9], Arvilla[8], Reuben[7], Moses P[6], John H[5], Yost[4], Bishop John[3], John (Hans[2]), Christian[1]) b: 3/25/2011

11ab. Coleson King[11] (Scott[10], Darrel[9], Arvilla[8], Reuben[7], Moses P[6], John H[5], Yost[4], Bishop John[3], John (Hans[2]), Christian[1]) b: 9/26/2008

11ac. Truett King[11] (Scott[10], Darrel[9], Arvilla[8], Reuben[7], Moses P[6], John H[5], Yost[4], Bishop John[3], John (Hans[2]), Christian[1]) b: 2/19/2010

11ad. Lachlan King[11] (Scott[10], Darrel[9], Arvilla[8], Reuben[7], Moses P[6], John H[5], Yost[4], Bishop John[3], John (Hans[2]), Christian[1]) b: 8/25/2011

11ae. Zachary Garret King^{11} (Anthony^{10}, Darrel^9, Arvilla^8, Reuben^7, Moses P^6, John H^5, Yost^4, Bishop John^3, John (Hans^2), Christian^1) b: 4/2/1993

11af. Kayla King^{11} (Anthony^{10}, Darrel^9, Arvilla^8, Reuben^7, Moses P^6, John H^5, Yost^4, Bishop John^3, John (Hans^2), Christian^1) b: 11/2/1996

11ag. Hayden King^{11} (Anthony^{10}, Darrel^9, Arvilla^8, Reuben^7, Moses P^6, John H^5, Yost^4, Bishop John^3, John (Hans^2), Christian^1) b: 9/26/2003

11ah. Samantha King^{11} (Anthony^{10}, Darrel^9, Arvilla^8, Reuben^7, Moses P^6, John H^5, Yost^4, Bishop John^3, John (Hans^2), Christian^1) b: 10/2/2006

11ai. Silas King^{11} (Anthony^{10}, Darrel^9, Arvilla^8, Reuben^7, Moses P^6, John H^5, Yost^4, Bishop John^3, John (Hans^2), Christian^1) b: 10/2/2006

11aj. Drew Michael Westover^{11} (Crystal^{10}, Delmar^9, Arvilla^8, Reuben^7, Moses P^6, John H^5, Yost^4, Bishop John^3, John (Hans^2), Christian^1) b: 5/24/2000

11ak. Hunter Lee Benfer^{11} (Crystal^{10}, Delmar^9, Arvilla^8, Reuben^7, Moses P^6, John H^5, Yost^4, Bishop John^3, John (Hans^2), Christian^1) b: 9/10/2008

11al. Chase Benfer^{11} (Crystal^{10}, Delmar^9, Arvilla^8, Reuben^7, Moses P^6, John H^5, Yost^4, Bishop John^3, John (Hans^2), Christian^1) b: 11/2/2010

11am. Megan Nichole King^{11} (Amy^{10}, Delmar^9, Arvilla^8, Reuben^7, Moses P^6, John H^5, Yost^4, Bishop John^3, John (Hans^2), Christian^1) b: 7/1/1996

11an. Hanna Marie King[11] (Brent[10], Delmar[9], Arvilla[8], Reuben[7], Moses P[6], John H[5], Yost[4], Bishop John[3], John (Hans[2]), Christian[1]) b: 5/17/2006

11ao. Brooke Elizabeth King[11] (Brent[10], Delmar[9], Arvilla[8], Reuben[7], Moses P[6], John H[5], Yost[4], Bishop John[3], John (Hans[2]), Christian[1]) b: 5/22/2008

11ap. Timothy Yi King[11] (Justin[10], Titus[9], Pauline[8], Reuben[7], Moses P[6], John H[5], Yost[4], Bishop John[3], John (Hans[2]), Christian[1]) b: 11/21/2012

11aq. Hayden Thomas Snyder[11] (Carmine[10], Daniel[9], Pauline[8], Reuben[7], Moses P[6], John H[5], Yost[4], Bishop John[3], John (Hans[2]), Christian[1]) b: 6/18/2000

11ar. Hunter Daniel Snyder[11] (Carmine[10], Daniel[9], Pauline[8], Reuben[7], Moses P[6], John H[5], Yost[4], Bishop John[3], John (Hans[2]), Christian[1]) b: 12/30/2003

11as. Brady Nathaniel King[11] (Nathan[10], Daniel[9], Pauline[8], Reuben[7], Moses P[6], John H[5], Yost[4], Bishop John[3], John (Hans[2]), Christian[1]) b: 4/15/2006

11at. Austin Daniel King[11] (Nathan[10], Daniel[9], Pauline[8], Reuben[7], Moses P[6], John H[5], Yost[4], Bishop John[3], John (Hans[2]), Christian[1]) b: 9/1/2007

11au. Ava Summer King[11] (Nathan[10], Daniel[9], Pauline[8], Reuben[7], Moses P[6], John H[5], Yost[4], Bishop John[3], John (Hans[2]), Christian[1]) b: 8/2/2010

11av. Rivers C. King[11] (Jacob[10], John[9], Pauline[8], Reuben[7], Moses P[6], John H[5], Yost[4], Bishop John[3], John (Hans[2]), Christian[1]) b: 12/23/2012

11aw. Reese Goss[11] (Mark[10], Richard[9], Lola[8], Reuben[7], Moses P[6], John H[5], Yost[4], Bishop John[3], John (Hans[2]), Christian[1])
b: 2008

11ax. Delaney Goss[11] (Mark[10], Richard[9], Lola[8], Reuben[7], Moses P[6], John H[5], Yost[4], Bishop John[3], John (Hans[2]), Christian[1])
b: 2010

Generation 12

12a. Cooper James Auker[12] (Kyle[11], Elizabeth[10], Patricia[9], Elmer[8], Reuben[7], Moses P[6], John H[5], Yost[4], Bishop John[3], John (Hans[2]), Christian[1]) b: 2/1/2010

12b. Cohen Jay Patterson[12] (Ashlee[11], Angela[10], Patricia[9], Elmer[8], Reuben[7], Moses P[6], John H[5], Yost[4], Bishop John[3], John (Hans[2]), Christian[1]) b: 6/12/2007

12c. Sierra Zuch[12] (Jessica[11], Pamela[10], Peggy[9], Elmer[8], Reuben[7], Moses P[6], John H[5], Yost[4], Bishop John[3], John (Hans[2]), Christian[1]) b: 10/2/2010

12d. Roary Zuch[12] (Jessica[11], Pamela[10], Peggy[9], Elmer[8], Reuben[7], Moses P[6], John H[5], Yost[4], Bishop John[3], John (Hans[2]), Christian[1]) b: 3/8/2012

12e. Lincoln Michael Zuch[12] (Jessica[11], Pamela[10], Peggy[9], Elmer[8], Reuben[7], Moses P[6], John H[5], Yost[4], Bishop John[3], John (Hans[2]), Christian[1]) b: 5/10/2013

12f. Jeffrey Edward Dye[12] (Stephanie[11], Tracy[10], Susan[9], Elmer[8], Reuben[7], Moses P[6], John H[5], Yost[4], Bishop John[3], John (Hans[2]), Christian[1]) b: 9/2/2013

Appendix 1

A Story of St. Joder by Ben Yoder

In the spirit of celebrating St. Joder's Day, I offer the following summary of a story I've concocted, but first, a few words.

1) This is a work of fiction. Do not mistake it for anything claiming to be history. I've incorporated some historical details and tried to include some things from the paintings on the walls of St. Joder Kappelle, but it's mostly just my imagination. As a matter of fact, the whole story of the Theban Martyrs has been called into question since the Reformation, and there's a lot of evidence it never happened. Even so, it's fun to tell a good story about it.

2) This is only a summary of the story. If I (or hopefully anyone else) were to write or orally re-tell the story, I would add a lot of description and dialog and so forth. The summary is just to give an idea of how the story might go, and isn't intended to be used verbatim. You could try, but I don't think it would make for a very good story.

3) I give permission to anyone who wishes to use this story for their own purposes, either to be written or re-told. The only thing I ask is that, like all good storytellers, you make it your own. If there's something you don't like or would do differently, add, delete, or switch things around to your heart's content. All good storytellers changes stories before they pass them along.

So here's the story summary . . .

Forgiveness in Your Bones

St. Joder is traveling in the Rhone river valley near Agaunum, in the Roman province of Alpes Graiae et Poeninae, in the mid 360's AD. He is traveling from his home base of Octodurum (modern Martigny) down to Genava (modern Geneva) on church business. Traveling with him is his dog Ossy, a skinny, bony mutt he took in. During a storm, he seeks shelter in a mountain cave. He has a vision of a Roman legion commander who has been slain. He looks Egyptian from his features, and standing behind him in the shadows are two other officers. The vision doesn't speak but just looks at him in mute appeal. St. Joder asks how he will know the cause of the soldier's death. The vision points to St. Joder's dog and fades away.

After the storm is over, St. Joder finds his way into the town of Agaunum. This town, unlike others in the province, has never had a Christian congregation, and has stubbornly resisted any traveling evangelists. St. Joder begins to ask around about any legionnaires who died recently there. At first, the townspeople deny knowing anything about it, but St. Joder has a feeling that they aren't telling the truth. He keeps checking until an old man, toothless and almost senile, mutters something about "them getting what they deserved." He won't say any more.

The next morning St. Joder prepares to leave but can't find his dog. He searches all over until the dog turns up-- chewing on an old dry human thigh bone. He finds the place where the bone comes from, it's a very old mass grave-- hundreds, perhaps thousands of people are buried there. He confronts the townspeople, whose leader is a large man named Lucius. The townspeople become violent and attack him, beating him into unconsciousness and leaving him for dead. He is awakened by Ossy licking his face. He continues on his trip to Genava.

On his way back, several weeks later, he gets word that Agaunum has been struck by a plague. He rushes to the town. He learns Lucius's home has several members struck down with disease. St. Joder goes to Lucius's home and prays. Each person he prays for is healed. He prays for the town as a whole and the plague stops.

Afterwards, Lucius and several others ask St. Joder why he would help them. He explains-- Christ's parable of the unforgiving servant, Christ forgiving the soldiers who nail him to the cross, Stephen forgiving those who were stoning him. He explains how God's forgiveness for his sins frees him to forgive all others. You can't help it-- it's almost like something in your bones. They ask for his forgiveness for what they did to him and he freely gives it.

Lucius leads the townspeople in accepting the gospel and converting to Christ. Lucius then reveals what really happened almost 80 years before: the story of the Theban Martyrs. (A legion of some 6,000 soldiers is from Thebes in Egypt and is entirely composed of Christians. When they refused to attack and kill fellow Christians, and refused to join in emperor worship, Emperor Maximian, the junior emperor to Diocletian, is enraged. Twice he orders decimation-- killing every 10th soldier-- but they are steadfast, and finally the emperor orders the death of the entire legion, including its commander, Mauritius.)

Lucius reveals that the people of that town (their grandparents and great grandparents) had willingly participated in the massacre. They did it for many reasons: hatred of Christians, prejudice against Egyptians, greed for owning and re-selling the legion's weapons and supplies, and anger at the Roman government for the way it was slowly crumbling. The bodies were buried in several mass graves and accounts of the whole event were suppressed. The guilt and fear had been like a cancer in everyone's hearts. Lucius asks if God could ever forgive them. St. Joder says if God could forgive the whole world its sin, theirs was but a tiny part of that. He leads them in prayer for forgiveness.

The townspeople wish to do something to balance out what happened. St. Joder suggests they build a church near the massacre site so that praise to God would rise in place that had known only death. They agree to do so.

In time, the town of Aguanum will change its name to St. Maurice (also spelled Moritz), and 4 cathedrals, 598 churches and 74 towns would eventually carry that name. The Theban Legion would never be forgotten.

That night St. Joder sees the soldiers again in a dream. This time they are healed and smiling.

Appendix 2

St. Joder and the Bell by Ben Yoder 2003

The records are scanty and the facts few. We don't know the date or place of his birth. We know nothing of his family or his education or the cause of his death. What we do know comes to us from Switzerland, from a time before Switzerland existed, when it was the torn edge of an empire slowly disintegrating under its own weight. The information we have starts with his name. It is recorded in several forms. In the 4th century Vulgate Latin of his day, his name as Theodorus.

To the Franks and Burgundians, whose newly adopted Latin would in time become French, his name is recorded as ThoduleAnd among the Germanic Alemanni tribesmen he was called Theoderic (pronounced thi-YOder-ric), which they quickly shortened to just Joder (pronounced yo-der), and by that name he was most widely known in the Middle Ages. Eventually he would become St. Joder, but in his own lifetime people knew him simply as Bishop Joder. For this is one of the crucial facts we have: he was indeed a bishop, a leader of the Christian community that existed in the Pennine Alps, in the towns strung along the River Rhone as it carved its way between the mountains. We know his seat of office was in Octodurum, today's Martigny, but he also labored for many years upriver in the town of Sitten (in French, Sion, and Latin, Sedunum). It's a quiet place, a town gathered around two up thrust hillocks. The people of Sitten will tell you today that there aren't many facts known about their patron saint, but this has endured: "Bishops come and bishops go," they say, "but none was as faithful and loving and holy a man as St. Joder."

One fine spring morning St. Joder, as had been his habit all his long years, rose before dawn and hiked a short way into the mountains that towered on either side of the Rhone river valley to find a place to pray. There in the fresh air and soaring alpine majesty the old white haired man could feel the divine

101

presence like nowhere else. His heart was troubled that morning because the work of rebuilding the church destroyed nearly 80 years before under Diocletian's persecution was going slowly. There seemed to be something that burdened the hearts of the people there, something that made the task of bricks and mortar harder than it should be, something that stunted and weakened the message of the faith he proclaimed. And so when he reached a particularly favorite meadow, it was with a heavy heart that he settled beside a boulder to pray. Just before he bowed his head he glanced around, and that's when he saw the Bell.

It was a stunning sight, to say the least, the most obvious reason being that, as one might expect, there aren't any bells high in the Alps on glorious spring days, or any other days for that matter. To add to that, the Bell appeared to be hanging in the entrance to a small cave in the mountainside, a cave that St. Joder had never seen before even though he had prayed many times in this very place. And to top it all off, this was no ordinary bell. St. Joder had seen bells before, but those were crudely made of thin iron sheets beaten together, and carried in the hand, and this Bell—well, this Bell was magnificent: slightly taller than a grown man and made of radiant burnished brass glowing in the morning sun like the Trump of God itself. It didn't take a great deal of thought before St. Joder was on his feet to get a closer look.

The Voice didn't speak until he was within ten feet of the bell, and then the words went right through him like a cleansing wind, a wind that seemed to blow from the very presence of the Bell itself.

"My son, my son, remove your shoes, for you are standing on holy ground."

This brought St. Joder to a complete halt, and without thinking he was kneeling and starting to unlace his shoes. Then he hesitated.

The Voice spoke again, and somehow the words seemed to speak with a father's smile. "No, no, my son, I am not constrained to burning bushes or the mouths of donkeys. It is true. Today I speak to you from this bell."

St. Joder immediately bowed completely to the ground and removed his shoes as fast as he could get them off. With a voice made weak from the weight of the moment, he remembered the correct response. "Speak, Lord, for Thy servant listens."

"Prepare yourself, for I have a task for you to do. Your path will end in a test like nothing else you have faced before. But when I give a task, I also give gifts. For you this day, I have the Gift of Hearing. Now, speak to the bell, my son, and command it to ring."

St. Joder felt bewildered and hesitated.

"Speak! Command the bell to ring!" And the Voice had the weight of mountains in its dominion.

"I, uh, I command you, O Bell, to ring." It was not exactly spoken in the most overpowering tone of authority, but it was audible. Give it that much.

Bong!

The sound reverberated down the mountains and across the valley, a golden sound that washed over the land like the waters of the Flood of Noah.

BONG!

The sound enveloped St. Joder and carried him on its curling wave. Light flooded his senses until he almost felt dissolved in it, liquefied and dispersed.

BONG!

Warmth. Oh the warmth. It filled him to the depths and heights of him. It was love, pure, incandescent and vast. To the end of his days, he never forgot this moment when the world was right and perfect.

He almost cried when it ended. The world faded and returned to the dullness of a bright spring day. Except . . . except for an echo of warmth that settled — that settled around his ears. He frantically clasped his hands to the side of his head. His ears were the same. He could feel no difference. Yet — what was that?

He looked up. The clouds, great fleecy herds of them, were sprawled across the sky and *droned* in a sleepy, contented mumble born of moisture and sun as they migrated towards the horizon. He looked around him. The mountains were rumbling back and forth in deep grinding voices that went so low he felt them vibrating through the soles of his feet, muttering in tones of basalt and granite and magma that bubbled far below. He looked down. Down in the valley the river swirled a bright, clattering, chattering language, ever changing, ever varied, eternal river stone language. The whole world talked and bawled and gossiped and murmured at the top of its lungs.

Then it faded. Not completely, but just to the edge of consciousness, like the sounds at the fringes of dreams, waiting.

"My son, go now. Be ready. I will call at a time you do not expect."

The Bell was beginning to fade as well, turning thin and insubstantial.

He surged to his feet. "Lord, wait! Will I ever see you again?"

"When that which is broken mends, my voice will awaken and drive all foes to flight."

St. Joder was left standing in an alpine meadow on a glorious spring day, staring at an empty cave. He stood for the longest time, and then bent to put on his shoes.

His life returned to normal, and that was a wearisome thing. Though he strained his ears, the world did not speak up, and it was back to the task of building and preaching and visiting and managing, until he began to wonder whether it had been some trick of wishing and bad digestion.

Through the swift alpine summer life went on until the grape harvest neared. That was when the disaster struck. Without warning the grape leaves turned black and fell from the vines, and the fruit wrinkled up and started to rot. In a land where wine is a daily beverage due to its ability to not spoil, the winter was suddenly looming as a long, cold, thirsty time.

St. Joder was taking a walk through the market, where the townsmen were meeting to commiserate and prepare for the upcoming dearth. Perhaps no one would be starving, but the winter was always a hard time which a few didn't make it through, and the loss of the wine crop only made it worse. The people were standing and talking between the stalls. His ears for no apparent reason suddenly began to feel warm.

"Over here, bishop!"

The old man stopped and looked around to see who had called him. No one in the market paid any attention to him. He started to continue on.

"We said over here, bishop! Don't walk by and ignore us!"

He stopped immediately and carefully looked the crowd over to see who it was. Perhaps someone was smiling, pulling a prank. No one seemed to be a likely candidate. But who would be calling him, and in a voice so dry and scratchy? It sounded like someone who had been left in a parched desert for far too long.

"Down here, bishop! On the table!"

The old man glanced down to see someone had laid down a large bunch of withered and half rotted red grapes on the table next to him.

"That's right! It's us! Pick us up. We have something to say."

St. Joder reached for the bunch, then looked up and muttered to himself,
"Mountains and rivers and clouds are one thing, but *spoiled grapes*? Is a man of my age to be listening to *grapes*?"

"Well, it doesn't have to be beams of light and angels with flaming swords every time, now does it? Just hold us close to your ear because all this shouting has almost worn us out, and we can't keep it up much longer."

Feeling more than a bit foolish, St. Joder lifted the bunch and held it close to his right ear. The people nearest him in the

106

marketplace caught sight of what he was doing and paused their conversations to watch. The bishop was a well-known and respected man, but this was unlike anything he had ever done. A widening pool of silence surrounded him as the old man held the bunch to his ear and nodded several times. Finally he put down the bunch and looked at the townspeople gaping at him.

"People of Sitten, listen to me! God has heard your cries! Bring to me every empty wine jar and vat and barrel you own. Every cask and flagon and jug and keg! Let nothing be left out. Bring them here to the marketplace now."

At first people took it as too fantastic to be obeyed, but then one woman rushed from her home with a wine jar, and then someone else did too, and that seemed to break the dam. Within a short time, several hundred vessels were lined up, every one empty and waiting.

St. Joder walked down the rows of vessels, and in each one he placed a dry and withered grape plucked from the bunch in his hand. When that ran out, he got another and continued until every single one from chest high barrels to small, plain earthen jars had a grape in it. He then stretched his arms out and prayed a short prayer.

Nothing happened.

St. Joder took a firm grip on his rising feeling of panic. The Lord wouldn't have led him this far to abandon him. He turned to look at the gathered faces. He saw the people, the ones he had preached to and persuaded and reasoned with, the ones that had seemed so stubborn and resistant to the message he brought, the ones that had almost worn him out with their silent rejection, and they were right there, waiting, their eyes and ears open, half expectant, half resistant. His heart swelled with the words he wanted to say.

"People, the Lord spoke of having faith as small as a mustard seed, or perhaps it might be as small as a — withered grape." And he was off and running. The words flowed from him like a stream in spring. He talked of the mustard tree growing from the tiny seed, and then moved to the Lord supplying miraculous wine at the wedding feast of Cana, and was winding up with the five loaves and two fishes feeding the five thousand when a collective gasp from the crowd interrupted him. He glanced down. Every single vessel was filled to the brim with rich, deep red wine, sparkling in the sun. His heart leaped inside him. He picked up a small cup near him and held it to his lips for a sip. The slow smile on his face told the whole story, and then he handed it to whoever was nearest. A buzz of excitement and then plain joy erupted from the crowd. And the following Sunday, there was a different mood at church.

No one ever forgot that day. For centuries to come, people would remember the day God restored the wine harvest with the best vintage anyone had ever known. St. Joder kept a small barrel for himself in the small quarters he had next to the church he was rebuilding, on the crest of one of the two hillocks. He was always generous with it, freely sharing cups of the wine with friends and travelers and beggars, whoever he met. "Here," he would say, "This will cheer your heart and give you strength." And people would walk away with a new sense of confidence and hope, a sparkle in their eye, ready to go on. As long as St. Joder lived, that barrel never ran dry, but always had more to share. When people asked him how he had known to do what he did that day, he would smile and reply, "Let's just say it doesn't always take beams of light and angels with flaming swords. Sometimes you just have to listen."

The cup smashed into the flagstones.

"Who vomited up that foul fluid?" The tinker gave St. Joder a blistering scowl. "What are trying to do, poison me?"

St. Joder was shocked into speechlessness. In the four years he had been giving people cups of wine from his barrel, no one had ever reacted like this. The tinker at his doorstep had looked grateful when he offered the wine. Then he had taken one small sip.

The bishop found his voice. "My good man, as God is my witness, I was offering you the best I had in my home. I, I cannot explain what would make you feel this way."

"Anyone would feel the way I do if someone offered them that wretched slop! It tasted like something scooped out of an open sewer." The man stood there for a minute, glaring at the bishop, is if daring him to contradict what he'd said. In the midst of his confusion, something began to tug at his attention. It almost felt like an itching in his ears.

"It burned and burned all the way down! It was like swallowing molten rock!" exclaimed a voice that was like the bellowing of a bull shaped into words. "No, no, you idiot! It was like sucking snake venom!" said a different voice, one that sounded deep and oddly grating on the nerves.

"Whatever it was, it almost killed us. Now shut your mouths and wait." This one was high and thin and seemed to slither.

St. Joder stared at the man in horror. It didn't take much for him to conclude what he was hearing — the man was possessed. There was one thing in all his long life that he had never faced, and that was demonic powers. He felt little desire to begin now.

"Please, Lord," he prayed silently to himself, "please, not that. Should a man of my age have to do this? Please, send someone else. Let this man go on his way."

Deep in his heart, St. Joder could feel an urging, a wordless command to confront what he was hearing, and not to flee. The scene flashed across his mind of the Apostle Paul facing the demon possessed girl at Philippi. With a blink and a deep feeling of misgiving, he knew what he had to do.

The old man reached out his hand, only slightly trembling, and spoke to the angry man on his doorstep.

"In the name of Jesus Christ, I command you to come out of him!"

That was all it took. The man immediately fell onto his back and began to writhe and scream. Three times a terrific convulsion shook him, accompanied by shrieking and half strangled words of anger and hatred, but in the end the man was lying quietly on his back.

St. Joder knelt beside the man and touched his shoulder. He looked into the man's eyes.

The man stared back, at first too stunned to speak, and then his face crumpled into tears. Racking sobs burst out, followed by words of thanks. St. Joder helped him sit up and held him in an embrace until the sobs subsided, then got him to his feet and through the door into his home.

The man was later able to tell his story of how for years he had carried the demons inside him. They had forced him to do hideous things, until he had lost his family, his village and trade, and could only wander from place to place eking out a living as a tinker. There were many tears. St. Joder wrote a letter to the elder of the congregation near the man's village, telling what had happened and asking him to assist the man in putting the pieces of his life back together. There were more tears at this, but near the end the man accepted another cup of St. Joder's wine, and this time it had the usual effect. The man left, smiling and waving over his shoulder.

"Oh Lord," St. Joder prayed as he waved back, "thank you for getting me through this, but I ask you to not make me deal with this kind of thing again." He closed his door, but just before it was tight he heard a dark mutter, like a shadow flitting across his heart.

Several days later, St. Joder was hurrying home late in the evening, anxious to be indoors before the daylight failed. He came to the main bridge over the river Rhone and was at the crest when the world began to speak again, but this time in a different tone of voice. The river began chattering in its way while the stones of the bridge and the boulders in the river below vibrated their slow thoughts, but all of their speech was thick and clotted, filled with deep-seated rage and disgust, like someone forced to wade chest deep in sewage, like someone witnessing a crime and not able to do a thing about it. The force of it almost made him stumble. He stopped and looked around, and that's when he spotted them. Crouched on three boulders in the middle of the river below were three dark, hideous forms, like misshapen beasts. He could almost see the river trying to curl away from touching them, the boulders shifting and trying to be free of their foul weight.

"Are our forces ready to strike, Abbraxas?" The voice was familiar, like an animal grunting and bellowing human speech.

"Yes, yes, for the tenth time, yes, you idiotic lump of muscle. Azazel, strike Buer again until he learns to listen." This voice was high and thin.

There followed some thumping and snarling and jumping from rock to rock until the forms were at rest again.

"I just want to hear the good news, Abbraxas!" said the animal voice.

"You will hear it, imbecile. How will we not hear it? Every Servant on earth and below will roar with pleasure when the knife strikes our great enemy."

A deep and grating voice like heavy claws dragged across a slate spoke up. "Sweet blood! Sweet pain! I can almost smell it now. And then? What about us? Will we have our revenge on the simpleton who cast us from our mount? I want to squeeze him till his heart pops!"

"On that, we will have to await word from Down Below. I too hunger for it, Azazel. It may be years until we get a new mount, years of waiting in the shadows. We owe it all to you, Buer, you cretin! Strike him again, Azazel!"

There was more howling and flailing.

"Mercy, Abbraxas! Mercy! I could not stand that vile concoction our mount had swallowed."

"Neither could Azazel or I, but did we relax our grip? No, it was you! You, you oaf! If you cannot help keep the mount pinched tighter, then I shall recommend to Lord Adramalech that you be given an earthworm next. Perhaps then you will learn to ride your mount with proper control."

"Mercy, Abbraxas, mercy! I swear by the Lake of Fire it will not happen again. I beg of you not to say anything to Lord Adramalech. I will be a Servant crouched at your feet, learning

112

from your glory all the craft I can contain, serving you until the end of time itself."

"Silence! I grow weary of the sound of your voice. Let us be away now. Loss of a mount doesn't mean loss of discipline, and we have much more patrolling yet to do. Perhaps some small crumb of success can follow our noisome defeat."

With that the three forms melted away and St. Joder was left standing on the bridge with his stomach churning and his mouth dry.

That night St. Joder lay in his bed, tossing and turning, unable to sleep. He almost wished he hadn't received the Gift of Hearing. What action was being planned? Who was the great enemy? What might they do to *him* in revenge for the loss of the tinker? These thoughts chased each other around and around until sleep was hounded far away. At last he got up and opened his window, hoping some air might clear his mind. The peaceful village lay spread out around the hillocks, illumined by a full moon.

The large horned owl landed with a muffled whoosh on the ledge, startling the old man. "Don't be afraid, Theodorus," the owl said, after the bishop had regained his composure, "but listen carefully. I bring an important word. Tonight someone seeks to take the life of the Bishop of Rome."

"Damasus? Someone wants to kill him?"

"You must warn him, Theodorus. The assassin wears a goat's head amulet and walks with a limp. Warn Damasus!" And then the owl was off in a flurry of wings.

"Wait! Rome? How will I get there?" But it was too late. St. Joder was left in turmoil. Damasus . . . the man who had risen high to hold the see of Peter himself, had become the most honored and respected bishop in the empire, and some said the true leader of all Christians everywhere. And one of St. Joder's oldest friends. The thought of someone trying to take Damasus's life almost made him ill. And it would take weeks of travel to get there. How could he ever reach the city tonight? St. Joder sat down on his bed, his head in his hands.

"Lord, if you wish me to do this, if that is why you sent word to me, then provide me with a way, if that is your will."

Three harsh voices sounded faintly through his window. Coming to his feet again, St. Joder peered out into the moonlight. There, around the side of the hillock his home and the slowly rebuilding church occupied were three dark forms bounding and flying and bouncing from tree to rock to ground. As before, they appeared to be spending as much time arguing and attacking each other as they did cooperating. Their presence suddenly filled St. Joder with rage.

"How dare this abominable spawn befoul my town! Have I not done everything I can think of to lead people into light? And now these denizens of hell think they can ruin everything I've worked for!"

A thought flashed across his mind. It made him turn pale. It was mad, some might say, but it had a chance of getting him to Rome *and* ridding Sitten of the demons, although the risks would be horrifying. "Is there an open door here?" he whispered to himself. "If so, may I have the strength to grip it with both hands."

Before he could lose his nerve, he leaned out of his window and called out, "Foul minions of darkness, come to me here, if you dare!"

114

Their kind could not resist such words, eager as they are to advance in rank and reluctant to show any sign of fear before others of their kind. They also harbored a violent hatred toward the old man that pulled them in as well. Instantly the three gathered at his window, crouched at the casement, reeking a fetid odor of equal parts rotting meat and heated dung. "Speak, old fool, and don't waste our time," said the smallest of the three.

"I have a task for you to do. Which of you is the fastest?"

"That would be me," said the tallest of the three, clapping together immense bat like wings. The spirit had the feet of a monstrous bird, but the head of a hairless goat, while his body was covered with what looked like open sores. St. Joder knew his voice: harsh and discordant, a pain to the ears. "I am Azazel, and I travel swifter than grief."

"And which of you is the strongest?"

The broadest had been squatting like a toad. "I am," he said, and St. Joder recognized this voice too—an animal's bellowing. He straightened up. His limbs were as thick as tree trunks and dense with coiling muscle. Glistening black scales were everywhere. He opened his wide, lipless mouth and a tongue as long as a python twirled about before being pulled back in. "Buer is stronger than a minotaur."

"And which of you is the smartest?"

"That is me, beyond all doubt," said the smallest, pushing between the two on either side. It was pale, like a stillborn infant that never saw the sun, and stood the size of a boy. Its skull was grotesquely swollen to three times normal size, and its small, squinting eyes glinted with malice. "I am Abbraxas, the commander of these two, and only Lord Amon is craftier than I." This one had the high, slithering voice. "What do you propose?"

"Azazel must carry me to Rome and back. Buer may assist if Azazel so chooses. You, Abbraxas, will wait here. If you bring me back after the rooster crows, then all three of you must leave Sitten and never return."

"And if we return before the rooster crows?" Abbraxas asked. "What will you offer us that will entice us into this bargain?"

St. Joder paused for just a second, and desperately searched his mind for an alternative, but there was only one thing he knew of that would motivate them. "You may have me for your new mount, and my soul upon my death."

All three roared with pleasure.

"I can taste your soul already, senile fool," crowed Abbraxas. "But what's this about roosters? How do I know you won't betray us with some hidden trick?"

"That's why you will stay here. I will get my rooster and you get yours. Both will be in your keeping. You can personally make sure I do nothing to unfairly influence either one. Both must crow together to end the deal. So what is your answer?"

Abbraxas's eyes glittered. "You will not believe what I will make you do once we take possession of your body. Yes, it's a deal, but—if you try anything, if you deliberately drag your heels or purposely cheat in any way, then we get your soul, no questions asked. So what is *your* answer?"

"Cheat? Isn't that more a specialty of your kind? *I* propose that if you try to cut my journey short without accomplishing its goal or returning me here, then you will leave Sitten forever, whether we are back in time or not, understood?"

"Perfectly. Now go get your rooster."

St. Joder ran to gather up sleeping King David, his fine white rooster. Abbraxas disappeared to reappear moments later with a skeletal bird that retained only a few straggling black feathers and smelled of rotting flesh. It stirred briefly in his hands. Both birds, sleepy but awake, were placed on the town wall near the northwest tower, with Abbraxas watching from a short distance.

Azazel knelt before St. Joder. "Now, human, sit on my back and don't fall off."

Even though the demon's open sores made the old man's skin crawl, he carefully seated himself on the thing's shoulders, careful not to touch anywhere with his bare hands, and they were off into the night. Under other circumstances, the trip would have been the glory of a lifetime, but as it was he barely noticed as they soared high above the Alps and then down the length of Italy. Long before he expected the trip to end, they had landed outside the large villa on the outskirts of Rome where Pope Damasus lived.
"Be quick about your business, old fool. If I think you're playing a trick, I will mount you *immediately*, whether the others are present or not." Azazel smiled most unpleasantly.

"Just wait here. I won't be long." St. Joder hurried into the building.

It didn't take long for St. Joder to rouse the entire household. Soon dozens of servants, guards and underlings were rushing about. Finally Damasus himself, in a richly ornamented, though hastily donned, robe was ushered in. He seated himself in a large, elaborately carved chair, a man in his early seventies with a long, full beard, a sizeable paunch, and heavy bags under his eyes.

"My old friend, Theodorus, this is quite a surprise. Sit here beside me." For all his years, his voice had not lost its rich, deep baritone. A hand heavy with rings patted a bench beside him. St. Joder took the seat. "Now, what brings you here so suddenly in the middle of the night?"

"I cannot stay long, Blessed Damasus, so I will be brief. Is there anyone in your household who limps?"

Damasus's eyebrows shot up. "Well, yes, as a matter of fact, there is." Every eye in the room turned toward a guard officer. "My captain, Marcus Juventus here, has limped since my struggle with Ursinus all those years--"

Before he could finish his sentence, the man ripped his dagger from its scabbard and threw himself at the pontiff, screaming curses. He landed at the feet of Damasus, only to be overpowered and subdued by guards and servants. When the confusion and shouting finally settled down, and the visibly shaken Damasus had composed himself, St. Joder continued.

"If there is any doubt of this man's mission, check beneath his tunic. You will find he is wearing a goat head amulet." A quick look revealed this, causing the man to scream once more and thrash in the grip of the men holding him, and the servants and underlings to mutter and give St. Joder long, dark looks.

"I was warned of this by a miraculous messenger, and only tonight was I able to reach you with word of it."

The servants and underlings began to talk loudly until Damasus stood up and commanded the captain to be dragged away and tied up, then dismissed everyone back to their beds.

"Theodorus, come with me."

They walked down a corridor lined with murals and marble busts. Mosaics depicting the miracles of Christ covered the floor. "My heart is still pounding from what just happened back there, Theodorus. I need a breath of fresh air to calm my nerves." They walked out into a portico leading to one of the gardens.
"How many years has it been, old friend?" "Since I saw you last? It's been a good ten years or more, perhaps when you consecrated me as bishop."

"No, no, since we were catechumens together."

"Oh — well, then it's been forty five years, at least."

"That long? Truly? That's what marks us as old, isn't it? The long ago is clearer than yesterday. I can still smell the ink and vellum of the looks at the scriptorium. I remember walking and laughing and debating with you, Theodorus. And riddling. Do you still like to ask riddles?"

A smile touched St. Joder's face. "Yes, once in a great while, and every time I do so I think of you. What was that one you made up about David? You could think them up faster than I, but mine were harder."

"Harder? I think not!" They both laughed. "Well, be that as it may, here I have another riddle. An old friend shows up suddenly and saves my life. How is it again that you got here?"

"Damasus, suffice it to say that the Lord sent a messenger to warn me. I wouldn't have believed anything else — and I would have had no other way to know."

"Hmmm, I guess not. It's a bit much to assume an enemy would just happen to tell a bishop out in — where are you, in Rhaetia?"

"Alpes Poeninae. The town of Sedunum."

"Yes, a small place, near the heathen Allemanni as I recall. Are you happy there, out at the edge like that?"

"The work is hard, my friend, but I am content."

"And this messenger from the Lord, he wasn't a mutual acquaintance of ours, was he?"

"Not at all. He was, shall we say, a wise old bird, but no one I had ever met before."

"And your journey here?"

"Aided by some recent, er, acquaintances, who have been — um, gracious — enough to let me travel with them. The message left me no time to wait for sunrise and my acquaintances leave me little time to linger here in your home." He folded his arms and gave him a small smile.

Damasus shot him a wary look. "That's it?"

"Yes, Damasus, old friend, that's it. For the sake of our friendship, I ask you to trust me when I do not describe more."

"I can see there's more to this riddle than I will solve tonight. Well, be that as it may, I am deeply in your debt. I would like to properly thank you. . .

" St. Joder laid a hand on his friend's arm. "Damasus, I'm not sure that's possible."

"Not possible? What are you talking of?" His eyebrows shot up, then drew together. "What do you say to a banquet? I'll have you know I have the most wonderful cooks in all Rome. One little Thracian in my employ makes the most delicate honey cakes between here and Armenia." He gave St. Joder a merry look. "And I'm well known among all the patrician families for my post-dinner entertainment."

"Regretfully, no, Damasus, but thank you anyway."

The pair walked through the gardens. From somewhere St. Joder could hear splashing water, and the scent of night blooming lilies came to him.

"Then what about a triumph down the streets of Rome? The City isn't what it was in times past, but I think you'll find the crowds are still large. We'll do it in my own chariot, with a team of six matched horses. What do you say?"

"That sounds . . . impressive, but I can't."

"Perhaps something a little less carnal and a bit more spiritual? What about a liturgy of thanks at the basilica? You'll love the changes I've instituted — we use our own Latin, now that so few people speak Greek anymore. I've added so much more color, with gold and silver vessels gleaming everywhere, sweet incense in thick clouds, good beeswax candles bright and numerous, vestments in a riot of colors and brass bells in every size and pitch."

"That also sounds quite . . . impressive, but no. I'm sorry."

"Theodorus, you are making it difficult for me to say thank you."

"Then just say it, and that will be more than sufficient."

"But I'm not someone who does things by half measure, *and*, I might add, I'm not used to people resisting the thanks of the Bishop of Rome, who occupies the Holy and Apostolic See of the Fisherman himself, and holds the keys of death and Hades. And especially not by bishops from obscure provinces." His narrowed his eyes and gave him a sharp look.

St. Joder looked back and took a deep breath. "As much as I respect who you are and what you've done here, Blessed Damasus, I am just a humble man from a small town, too old for all that sort of thing. And I have something that demands I leave soon. I truly, truly can't stay a moment longer than--"

They had reached the opposite side of the garden and there in an alcove it was before him—a bell. As tall as a grown man and made of burnished brass glowing as bright as the Trump of God itself. It stood on a small wooden base.

"Theodorus—a moment longer than . . . what?"

St. Joder ignored him and approached the bell, pausing for a moment, and then coming close enough to gently reach out and stroke the bell's surface. A memory of a high alpine meadow filled him. "Speak, Lord, for Thy servant listens," he muttered to himself. As if waking from a dream, he realized Damasus was at his side.

"Beautiful, isn't it, Theodorus? Paulinus, bishop of Nola, had that made for me." He paused and looked carefully at St. Joder. "I can see it truly has captured your heart like nothing else can. Well, that settles it. It's yours."

That snapped St. Joder's attention back to the Pope. "Damasus, I, I couldn't. . ."

"Nonsense. I'm getting very tired of hearing that. If you can't accept a gift of love, a gift of gratitude, for all the years of your faithful service, for your friendship, then something is severely wrong."

"Damasus, what will I do with it?"

"Do with it? Do with it? Why, build a tower for it on that church you're working on and put it at the top. Use it to call the faithful to prayer. Announce births, deaths and weddings. Warn of approaching enemies. And—I have specially blessed it. Its voice will drive away whatever evil lurks nearby."

At these words, all reservations in St. Joder's mind evaporated. He knew at a deep-down level that it was right to be here and to take this work of beauty home.

"All right then. I accept your gift."

"Wonderful, wonderful! I'll have my people arrange for a cart tomorrow."

"That won't be necessary. My, er, people are already able to get it back."

Damasus looked at him from under bushy brows knit close together. "Old friend, are you *sure* there isn't more to this riddle you'd like to tell me?"

123

"My companions are — very special, and someday, God willing, I'll tell you all about how I came to be here tonight, but for now let's just say they are a little shy and not exactly the social kind. Let me go find wherever they are and I'll make the necessary arrangements."

After one more long look, the pope agreed to let it go at that. He embraced St. Joder and wished him a good trip home. They chatted a bit as people do before leave taking, and then the old pontiff said a final good-bye and walked, somewhat sleepily, back to his bed.

With a flap of powerful wings, Azazel landed beside the bishop. "Finished, old fool? We have a journey ahead of us and no time to waste."

"Quite finished. But you'll be carrying both me and *that*." He pointed to the bell.

"What? WHAT? Do you expect me to be your beast of burden? What do you think I am, a donkey for you to load up and beat with a stick? I refuse!"

"Is this too much for you to carry? I didn't realize just how fragile you demons are. I'm so sorry."

"I am a Servant of the Eighth Degree, in the Second Cohort of Lord Adramalech, and was there when the High Lord Himself sang with the morning stars, and I am not *fragile*! But I will not be subjected to this indignity!"

"I see. Well then, I agree. You should never be so grossly is honored. I'll just have to make arrangements with Pope Damasus in the morning for transportation of the bell. Of course, you'll need to explain to Abbraxas why you didn't

124

return with me in time — it being such a humiliation and all. I'm sure he'll be very understanding and supportive."

The demon shook his fists at the night sky and vented a roar of pure rage. "Oh little speck of dung that you are, I shall so enjoy making your final days ones of vilest torment."

With that he sprang to the bell and picked it up by the cross beam it was hung from and hoisted it over his head in one smooth motion. "Get ready to ride, withered morsel. Your agony will be savored for centuries to come."

The demon began to tuck the bell under his arm, but immediately yanked it away, hissing in pain. "The accursed thing burns! No matter! Climb on my back — quickly!"

St. Joder once again gingerly sat astride the devil's shoulders. The creature launched himself into the air, grasping the bell once more by the wooden cross beam, and lurched heavily aloft, hauling it beneath him. The immense bat wings labored mightily until the Pope's home had dwindled away far below. The journey down had been a swift flight, but the return was much slower. The demon's wings beat, his lungs pumped like bellows, his whole body shuddered with the effort, but slowly they lost altitude and speed. It was when they neared the Alps, and St. Joder and Azazel looked up at the towering peaks with their snow-covered summits, that both knew it was beyond the demon's strength. At last they dropped to the earth.

"You did the best you. . ."

"Shut your mouth, mortal. This is not ended."

The demon stood, lifted his hands to his mouth and let loose a cry that was half scream and half roar. It went on and on for a minute or more until Azazel broke it off abruptly and cocked his head to one side. "Good. He comes."

They waited some time, long enough for St. Joder to begin to doze, when he was woken by rhythmic impacts jolting through the earth. They culminated in one final smash and there in front of them stood a black figure with arms and legs like tree trunks.

"I come. I COME!"

Barely able to stand any longer, Azazel wearily pointed at the bishop and his bell." Take them both, Buer."

The demon picked up the bell, and even though they caused a sizzle and a smoking when it touched his scales, he showed no signs of pain but turned it upside and wrapped his arms around it.

"Get in, human."

"What?"

Without further word, Buer picked up the bishop by the nape of his neck and placed him inside the bell.

"Get in and stay in."

With that, he bounded high into the air. The ensuing journey was one of soaring leaps that seemed to last forever, punctuated by bone jarring shocks as they returned to earth. St. Joder had to clutch the clapper to keep from being thrown out. The mountains didn't seem to slow the demon at all, but he just kept bounding over snowfields and boulders and ridges. It seemed to take forever, but in a shorter time than St. Joder realized, they came vaulting down the pass and into the valley of the Rhone. Just as there was beginning a hint of a pre-dawn flush to the east, the old man caught sight of the twin hillocks of home. He almost stopped breathing as his heart turned to lead. It would be very close.

"I COME! I COME!" Buer roared as he leaped one last time to cross the city walls, just barely high enough to make it. The dawn was on the verge of breaking over the horizon.

St. Joder frantically looked for the two roosters perched just below him on the northwest tower. There was Abbraxas with his arms around both, his fists clutched tightly around their heads. "Crow, King David, crow my little warrior!" he called out.

Without warning time froze.

The absolute silence and crystalline clarity of a world locked tight shocked the bishop. He stood in the upside down bell and looked about him in the eerie hush. Suddenly hovering in front of him was Abbraxas, holding the roosters under his arms and keeping their beaks tightly pinched between his fingers.

"You didn't think you were going to get away that easily, now did you, you feeble witted old failure? Did you think Abbraxas was just going to sit here and buff his nails while you gallivanted around Italy? Absolutely not! I'm a Servant of the Third Echelon and a protégé of Lord Moloch himself. If you're going to win this little wager, then you'll have to get by me first. I challenge you to a duel of wits! I don't think you can even go one round with me, but let's say the first one of us who can't answer the other's challenge is the loser. What do you say to that?"

"Why should I endure any further contest when it was never agreed to in the first place?"

"Just think of it as fair for fair for that little stunt with the bell. And don't think I'm going to release my hold on these birds' beaks any time soon. If you don't agree, well, I'll so enjoy making you perform the most perverse and cruel acts I can conceive of, and I can conceive of *many*, and then we'll have an eternity to think over what fun we had. So suit yourself, old cretin."

"All right, unclean spirit, I agree to your contest. Same stakes as before?"

"But of course. And I will start — of course. Answer this if you dare:

> *I'll die soon*
> *If I'm not soon fed,*
> *The hands I lick*
> *Will soon turn red.*
> *What am I?*

"You don't have a chance, dim-witted worm!"

Now St. Joder was accustomed to this kind of thing. He and Damasus had excelled in creating and solving these puzzles when they were young, and he had continued to delight in them throughout his life, asking them in gatherings of townsfolk through the long, cold winters. This one he hadn't heard before, so he began turning it over and over in his mind, mentally looking at it from every possible angle. He began to think of every animal he knew that might fit the description, but he also knew misdirection was the key — it might sound like an animal, but it was probably something else. Luckily, it didn't take long for him to deduce the answer.

"Did you think this one would truly stump me? You no doubt thought of this one because it's a thing you will be spending a lot of time around, when your master and you are consigned to the Lake of — Fire. The answer is fire."

Abbraxas growled deep in his throat. "Don't get so cocky, prune. That was a quick one to get us going, but I've got lots more to go. Now you ask one."

St. Joder thought for a bit, then started:
> When I'm still a baby, I lie sweet in the sun.
> When I'm in my middle years, I make you light hearted.
> When I grow old, I'm more valuable than I ever was.
> Who am I? "

That's another quick one to get us going."

St. Joder hadn't realized that these metaphors were harder than they looked when the creature answering was steeped in hatred, malevolence and terror. Abbraxas had to ponder so long St. Joder began to hope he'd get out of this contest sooner than he expected. But before he said anything, the answer came to the demon's mind.

"What else other than what you sots use to blot out your pain? The answer is wine."

St. Joder conceded that was the answer and prepared himself for the demon's next try.

"Let's try something a little more challenging then:"
> Torn out of my mother's dark womb,
> Burned in a fire and beaten many times,
> I've become a killer, hungry for meat and blood.
> What am I?

"Not exactly lying sweet in the sun, is it? Try that one!"

St. Joder struggled with it. The puzzle seemed like something a demon's warped mind would think of. He thought of all the

people he'd met in his lifetime who might fit that description —
soldiers and thieves and professional torturers. But he knew it
wasn't the obvious. It was more likely to be an object
personified. Then what objects are killers? He thought about it
and thought about it until Abbraxas began to stir and rub his
hands together, as if anticipating a win. At last, the old man
answered.

"I have it. I think it was the 'burned' and 'beaten' part that
helped me. The beaten and burned killers among us are the
weapons we make at the forge. The answer is iron."

Abbraxas seethed in discontent at this correct answer, but had
to wait for St. Joder's next one.

St. Joder took a deep breath.
> I live three lives.
> I'm light enough to embrace the heavens,
> I'm gentle enough to soothe a baby's skin,
> I'm harsh enough to split stones.
> Who am I?

This one stymied Abbraxas. The concept of gentleness and
harshness combined was hard, and the triune nature of this one
made him think of the Great Enemy, which he shied away
from. It was only after much effort that he hit on the answer.

"You thought you had me stumped, but not this time. What
exists in three forms? It's ice, steam and — water. The answer is
water."

St. Joder acknowledged that was the correct answer.

"Now that last one got me angry," the demon continued, "so
I'm going to give you one that I've been saving for a very long
time. It's one of my favorites:"

Then all thy feculent majesty recalls
The nauseous mustiness of forsaken bowers,
The leprous nudity of deserted halls –
The positive nastiness of sullied flowers.
And I mark the colors, yellow and black ,
Those fresco thy lithe, dictatorial thighs.

St. Joder could feel sweat gathering under his arms. He didn't have a clue what this one was. To gain time, he asked the demon to repeat it several more times, which he did with increasing surliness and speed. Abbraxas sensed St. Joder's discomfort.

"What's the matter? Did your head crack and the brains leak out? You're cracking all right, you miserable wretch, like an egg under a boot. You know what we're going to do to you first after all three of us mount you? We're going to destroy you in front of your own people. Maybe we'll make you drown a child during baptism. Wouldn't that be a hoot? We'll have you thieving and philandering and embezzling until your own congregation vomits you out. And then we're just getting started. Oh my, oh my, are we going to have fun with you."

During Abbraxas's tirade, St. Joder had begun praying under his breath. "Lord, give me a sign. Help me somehow. Anything! I'm in need of your help."

Responding to a wordless inner prompting, he looked to his right. The only thing he could make out was a cobweb along the edge of the wall. He stared at it for a few seconds while Abbraxas spewed more venom. Nothing else came to the bishop.

"That's it, Lord?" he prayed. "A *cobweb*? What use is that?"

Then a memory came to him of walking the road from Sitten to Geneva many years before and seeing a large spider web suspended between two bushes, and spotting a large spider at the center with—black and yellow legs!

"And I mark the colors, yellow and black, that fresco thy lithe, dictatorial thighs," he whispered to himself. Aloud, he shouted, "It's a spider! A *spider*, you vile travesty!"

Abbraxas took considerable time to cool down, but at last he was calm and coherent enough to listen. And that was fortunate for St. Joder because he was in need of a hard one, and nothing was coming to mind. As he was staring at Abbraxas and racking his mind, his white rooster began to stir in the demon's hands. The sight of the rooster brought back to St. Joder's mind one of the earliest puzzles he had ever been asked, from his boyhood when he was learning to spell and count.

"Since that last one was so special to you," St. Joder said, "I have one that I remember from long ago:
> *Five hundred begins it, five hundred ends it,*
> *Five in the middle is seen;*
> *The first of all letters, first of all numbers*
> *Take up their stations between.*
> *Join all together, and then you will bring*
> *Before you the name of an eminent king.*

Surely someone as wise as Lord Amon can figure this one out, can't he?" Abbraxas screwed up his face, paced back and forth (the roosters still firmly in his grip), and muttered and cursed. The volume and pace picked up as time trickled by. "I'll give you a good long time, but at some point you've got to answer." The demon was getting more and more frantic, trying to cudgel his wits into producing the answer. The pacing turned into goose stepping and stomping and finally leaping in one spot.

132

"No, no, no! I can get this one! No way is that puny, frail, ignorant little *human* going to stump me. I demand three guesses! Three guesses!" St. Joder sighed. "There wasn't anything said about three guesses, but all right, guess away." "A map." "Nope." "A carved inscription." "Sorry." They were down to the demon's last guess. He began to hiss like a nest of fifty cobras. He scowled till he almost cracked the rock in front of him.

"King Solomon!" "Wrong again!" Relief washed over St. Joder's heart like a river at flood stage. He knelt inside the bell, his knees giving way. A heartfelt prayer of thanks went up. "What is the answer? Prove to me there *is* an answer." "Of course. It's DAVID. D is five hundred. V is five. A, the first letter, and I, the first number, take up their stations between." With that the world unfroze. Buer came to a crashing halt beside the wall just a split second after the bishop's rooster, King David, began crowing lustily. Cock a doodle doo! Cock a doodle doo! COCK A DOODLE DOOOOOO! It startled the other skeletal black rooster into crowing as well. St. Joder hastily scrambled out of the bell just as the demon set it down. The earth had never felt so sweet under him as it did then. He raised his hands in exultation. "I will not be kept from your soul," Abbraxas screamed. "I don't care what wager we made. I don't care who got here before the rooster crowed. I don't care who couldn't answer the riddle. I spit on it all. I shall take your soul and I shall take it now!" Abbraxas levitated into the air and thrust out his arm toward the bell, causing it to rise as well. As he and the bell rose together, Buer leaped to the top of the walls. Over the walls came flapping Azazel, just arriving. The three continued to rise together higher in the air, taking the bell with them.

"Die, you worthless cur!" The little demon cocked back his arm and hurled the bell straight at St. Joder. The old man desperately lunged to one side as the bell crashed into the earth inches away from where he had been standing, shattering into dozens of gleaming shards. The sound was like the breaking of the world on Judgment Day. When the dust settled, all St. Joder could do was stare in stupefied horror at what remained of the glorious bell. How could this have happened? What would he do now? He slowly passed his hand over his face.

"Speak to the bell, bishop." St. Joder looked through his fingers in the early dawn light for who had spoken. People were stirring and leaving their homes, drawn by all the noise and commotion. The voice was thin and tiny. He looked down. There was a mouse near his foot looking up. "Lay hands on the pieces and speak them into wholeness, bishop. Do it now." Muttering under his breath about grapes and owls and now this, St. Joder knelt down beside the shards and extended his hands over them. This time his voice was steadier than it had been in alpine meadow. "In the name of the Lord of Hosts, I say to you broken pieces, be whole." St. Joder looked up. A small crowd had gathered. A collective gasp came from their throats as they watched the pieces stir. The fragments lifted into the air and fitted themselves together, coming into contact with a musical sound. Before everyone's eyes the cracks healed and the bell re-formed without sign of seam or dent. "I command you, oh Bell, to ring." The bell lifted higher and higher into the air, hovering a short distance away from the demons, who were still watching.

Bong!

Its deep throated tolling was like the shout of Gabriel come to call God's people home.

BONG!

The sound was a cleansing wave washing the world right and clean. The demons screamed and covered their ears in agony, curling into balls and turning away.

134

BONG!

The people would never forget that day when the bell awoke and for just a moment heaven lay there within their grasp. With a piercing wail the three demons turned and fled, never to be seen in Sitten again. Slowly the bell returned to earth, lit by the early light into a shining glory. The old bishop's face was lit up almost as much. In his mind were the words he had heard in the meadow: *When that which is broken mends, my voice will awaken and drive all foes to flight.*

"People, come and see, come and see! This is a gift from the Bishop of Rome. Its voice saved my soul today and it is my fervent prayer that its sound will remind us of the mercy and protection that surrounds us every day. "He then proceeded to tell them of all the events that had happened that night from what he heard yesterday evening at the bridge to the bell in front of them now. Finally someone in the crowd asked, "What will we do with this bell now that it is here?"

"Do with it? Do with it? We'll build a tower on this church so the bell's voice will ring clear and loud from mountains to mountains across the Rhone. And never again will demons afflict this place." Indeed, they never did, not in the sixteen centuries since. From that day on there was a lightening of people's hearts, and a feeling of hope that was rare in those days stirred. What had been muffled and bound before now broke loose, and those who heard the voice of St. Joder took up the strength to learn and grow and build. The church rose quickly after that, and was filled with a joyous throng, and the shout when the tower was completed and bell hoisted into place must have reached around the world. The people say that after that whenever there was a raging storm, lightning or hail or wind, the bell's voice would ring out and the weather would disperse without harming anyone or anything. "Just listen for the bell," they would say, "and pray. God doesn't always need beams of light or angels with flaming swords to speak." And then they would look at Bishop Joder and smile. The old man would smile back *St. Joder's bell doesn't exist anymore, but when it was in Sitten, small chips of it were taken from time to time from around the edge and melted into new bellsat their casting. This was a custom so that the blessing of the original might be transferred to the new. There are many bells in churches of Switzerland today that claim they have a piece of St. Joder's bell in theirs. Names are little stories all tied up, some bound so tightly they almost can't be unknotted. The stories and legends of St. Joder, alongside the few facts, were circulated for centuries, and in time his name was attached to several places, including a hill. Still more centuries later, it became more and more common for people to choose surnames, and the families that had lived on Joder Hill for time out of mind naturally chose that name for themselves. Still more centuries yet, when a few families entered the Anabaptist movement and were viciously persecuted by both Catholic and mainstream Reformers, they chose to immigrate to the new world. These still spelled their surname Joder, but it didn't take more than a generation or two for it to be anglicized to Yoder, and that is how my name came to be. It is good to know your name has a story, a root that started long ago with one man who was faithful to God. If you travel to Sitten today, the people there will tell you they do not always remember everything about the life of that one man, but they will say, "Bishops come and bishops go, but none was as faithful and loving and*

holy a man as St. Joder." Sitten (Sion), Switzerland today.

Sources for Stories

The Catholic Encyclopedia.
http://www.newadvent.org/cathen/14014d.htm
Ecclesiology: A Study in Church History.
http://www.mcauley.acu.edu.au/~yuri/ecc/
A Little General History about Bells and Handbells.
http://www.handbells.org.au/genhist.htm
Ökumenisches Heiligenlexikon.
http://www.heiligenlexikon.de/index.htm?BiographienT/T
heodor_Teodul_von_Sitten.html
Spicer, Dorothy Gladys. 13 Jolly Saints, Ch. 3, "The Bishop's
Bell" (Switzerland).
Putnam Publishing Group (L). January, 1970.
Wikipedia, the free encyclopedia.
http://en.wikipedia.org/wiki/Pope_Damasus_I
Yoder Newsletter Online. Volume 1, Number 1 - May, 1983.
Volume 1, Number 2
October, 1983. Issue Number 6 - October 1985. Issue Number
7 - April, 1986.
http://www.yodernewsletter.org/YNL/vol01.html

Appendix 3
US Census
(Note: Arrows (⇨) point to ancestors)
John H. Yoder 1850

Page No. 127

SCHEDULE 1.—Free Inhabitants in *Spruce Hill Township* in the County of *Juniata* State of *Census* enumerated by me, on the 8th day of *July* 1860. *I. D. Howe* Ass't Marshal.

Post Office *Pleasant View*

		The name of every person whose usual place of abode on the first day of June, 1860, was in this family	Age	Sex	Color	Profession, Occupation, or Trade of each person, male and female, over 15 years of age	Value of Real Estate	Value of Personal Estate	Place of Birth, Naming the State, Territory, or Country				Whether deaf and dumb, blind, insane, idiotic, pauper, or convict	
1	2	3	4	5	6	7	8	9	10	11	12	13	14	
1		Margaret J "	8	f	M				Pa					1
2		Nancy P "	11	f					"					2
3		Anna M "	5	f					"					3
4		Wm B "	3	m					"					4
5		James C Gibson	30	m		Farmer	2500	600	"					5
6		Mary J "	38	m		"			"					6
7		Selina Y "	1	f					"					7
8	887 897	Thomas H Gibson	47	m		Farmer	5000	1200	"					8
9		Mary "	40	f		Housekeeper			"					9
10		James C "	12	m					"					10
11		David H "	10	m					"					11
12		James "	7	f					"					12
13		Zenas W "	4	m					"					13
14	888 892	Robert Patterson	57	m		Miller	3500	300	"					14
15		Nancy S "	53	f		Housekeeper			"					15
16		Isabella "	24	f		Teacher			"					16
17		John R "	21	m		Farmer			"					17
18		Mary A "	19	f		Teacher			"					18
19	889 893	John E Wilson	48	m		Farmer	6000	1500	"					19
20		Alice "	46	f		Housekeeper			"					20
21		Anna E "	19	f		Student			"					21
22		Robt W "	12	m					"					22
23	890 894	Anna H Seely	60	f		Lady			"					23
24		Alice Staynn	38	f		Housekeeper	400	800	"					24
25	891 895	Jas Ewing	26	m		Carpenter		250	"					25
26		Sarah "	27	f		Housekeeper			"					26
27		Samuel "	10	m					"					27
28	892 896	Joseph Kelly	64	m		M. D.	7000	2500	"					28
29		Anna B "	55	f		Housekeeper			"					29
30		Margaret "	31	f		"			"					30
31		John H "	25	m		Farmer			"					31
32		Joseph C "	22	m		Lawyer			"					32
33		Jas H Stewart	14	m		Student			"					33
34		George R "	12	m		"			"					34
35		Mary & Ira "	8	f	M				"					35
36	893 897	John Yoder	60	m		Farmer	8000	3000	"					36
37		Fanny "	47	f		Housekeeper			"					37
38		Catherine "	29	f					"					38
39		Sarah "	26	m		Farmer			"					39
40		Moses "	20	m		"			"					40

No. white males, | No. colored males, | No. foreign born, | No. blind, | No. idiotic, | No. convicts,
No. white females, | No. colored females, | No. deaf and dumb, | No. insane, | No. paupers,

Page No. 13

SCHEDULE 1.—Inhabitants in _Spruce Hill Township_, in the County of _Juniata_, State of _Penna_, enumerated by me on the _13th_ day of _August_, 1870.

Post Office: _Pleasant View_

R. C. _____, Ass't Marshal.

457

	Dwelling	Family	The name of every person whose place of abode on the first day of June, 1870, was in this family.	Age	Sex	Color	Profession, Occupation, or Trade	Value of Real Estate	Value of Personal Estate	Place of Birth								
1	104	101	Dobbs Thomas	46	M	W	Farmer	2600	1370	Penna								/
2			— Mary	44	F	W				//								
3			— Cameron	2	M	W				//								
4			Bowerman Mary	19	F	W	Domestic			//								
5	105	102	Shaw Samuel	70	M	W	at home	4000	1800	//								/
6			— Ann	65	F	W				//								
7		103	Beale Burch	37	M	W	Farmer		12	//								
8			—	22	F	W				//								
9			— Jane	1	F	W				//				/				
10			— Samuel	5	M	W				//				/				
11			— John	7	M	W				//				/				
12			— Nancy	13	F	W				//						/		
13			Freese Wm	14	M	W	Farm Hand			//				/				
14	106	104	Yoder Lucy	17	F	W	Keeping house			//								
15			— Neckel	14	M	W				//				/				
16			— Adaline	11	F	W				//				/				
17			Beck Maria	41	F	W	at home			//				/				
18	107	105	Shearer M. J.	60	M	W	Farmer	4100	3900	//								/
19			— Nancy	56	F	W				//								
20	108	106	Williams Joseph	51	M	W	Farmer	2000	260	//								/
21			— Anna	24	F	W				//								
22			— Washington	7	M	W				//								
23		107	Rogers Reuben	48	M	W	Farm laborer		100	//								
24			— Ann	40	F	W				//				/				
25			— Jane	9	F	W				//								
26			— Hess	7	M	W				//								
27			— Susan	6	F	W				//								
28			— Washington	4	M	W				//								
29			— Emily	2	F	W				//								
30	110	108	Yoder Moses	21	M	W	Farmer	2000	1000	//								/
31			— Sarah	24	F	W				//								
32			— Emma	1	F	W				//								
33	111	109	Rogers John	23	M	W	Farmer			//								/
34			— Euphemia	19	F	W				//								
35			— Miller	10	F	W				//								
36			— Joseph	13	M	W	Works on farm			Pa				/				
37	112	110	Harper Mary	50	F	W	Keeping house	3100	800	Pa								
38			— Elmira	20	F	W				Pa								
39			— Emma	14	F	W				Pa				/				
40			— Charles	8	M	W				Pa				/				

No. of dwellings 9 No. of white females 21 No. of foreign born. — 24,600 No. 18

No. of families 10 No. of colored males. — females. — Idiots. —

No. of white males 19 No. of blind. —

142

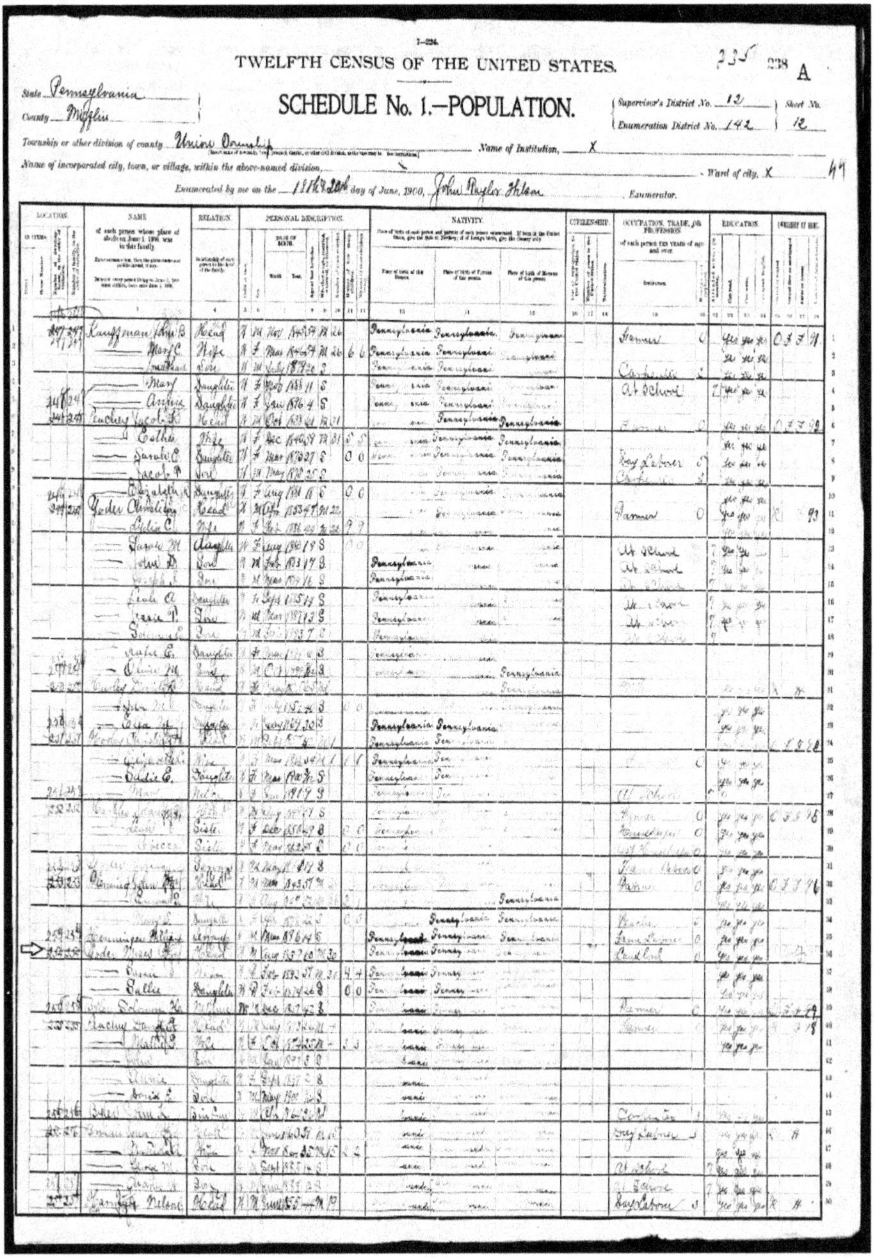

7—224.

TWELFTH CENSUS OF THE UNITED STATES.

SCHEDULE No. 1.—POPULATION.

235 238 A

State *Pennsylvania*

County *Mifflin*

Supervisor's District No. *13* Sheet No.

Enumeration District No. *142* *12*

Township or other division of county *Union Township* Name of Institution, *X*

Name of incorporated city, town, or village, within the above-named division, _____ Ward of city, X 44

Enumerated by me on the *11th 20th* day of June, 1900, *John Taylor Shlem*, Enumerator.

(Census population schedule — handwritten entries largely illegible)

144

Reuben Yoder 1900

Reuben Yoder 1910

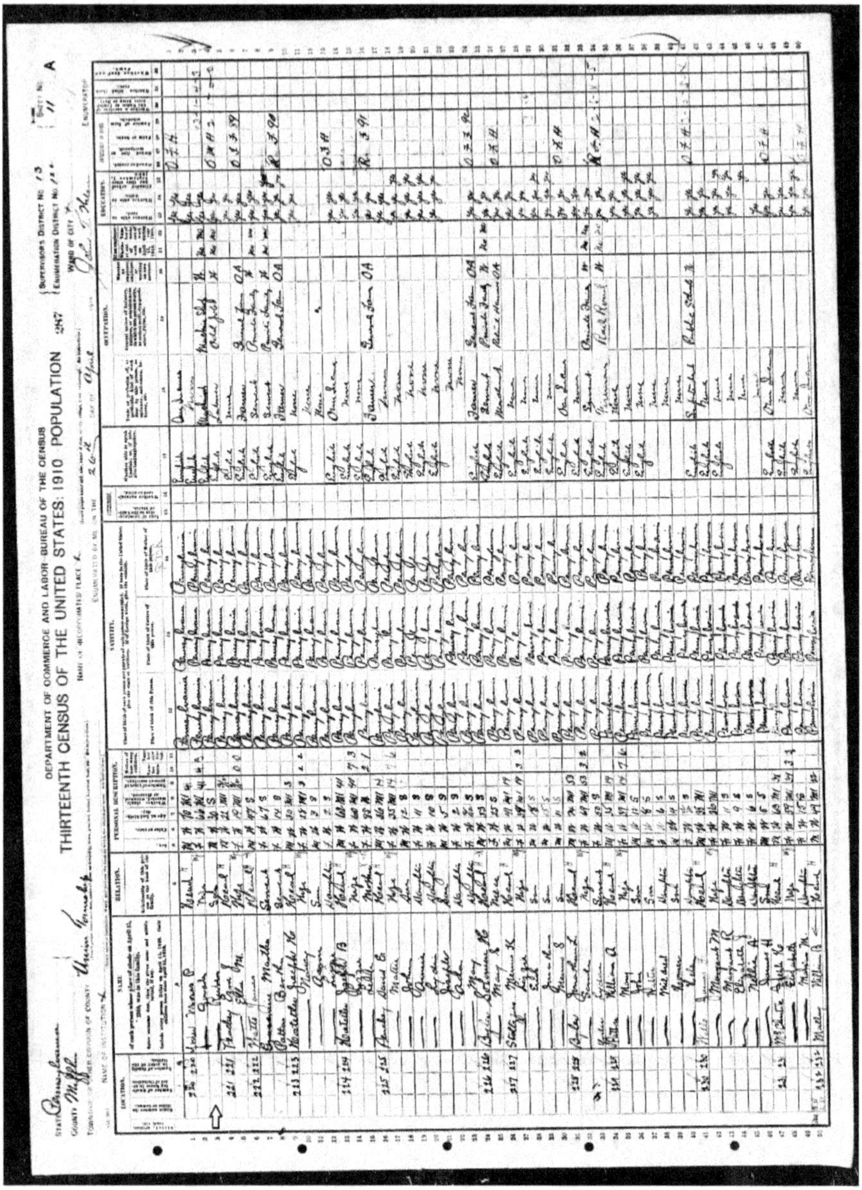
DEPARTMENT OF COMMERCE AND LABOR—BUREAU OF THE CENSUS

THIRTEENTH CENSUS OF THE UNITED STATES: 1910 POPULATION

Reuben K. Yoder 1920

Reuben K. Yoder 1940

148

7—224.

TWELFTH CENSUS OF THE UNITED STATES.

SCHEDULE No. 1.—POPULATION.

State _Pennsylvania_

County _Mifflin_

Supervisor's District No. _12_

Enumeration District No. _142_

Sheet No. _12_

Township or other division of county _Union Township_

Name of Institution, _X_

Name of incorporated city, town, or village, within the above-named division _X_

Ward of city _X_

Enumerated by me on the _26th_ day of June, 1900, _John Rayler Wilson_, Enumerator.

286 B

Mary M. (Zook) Yoder 1910

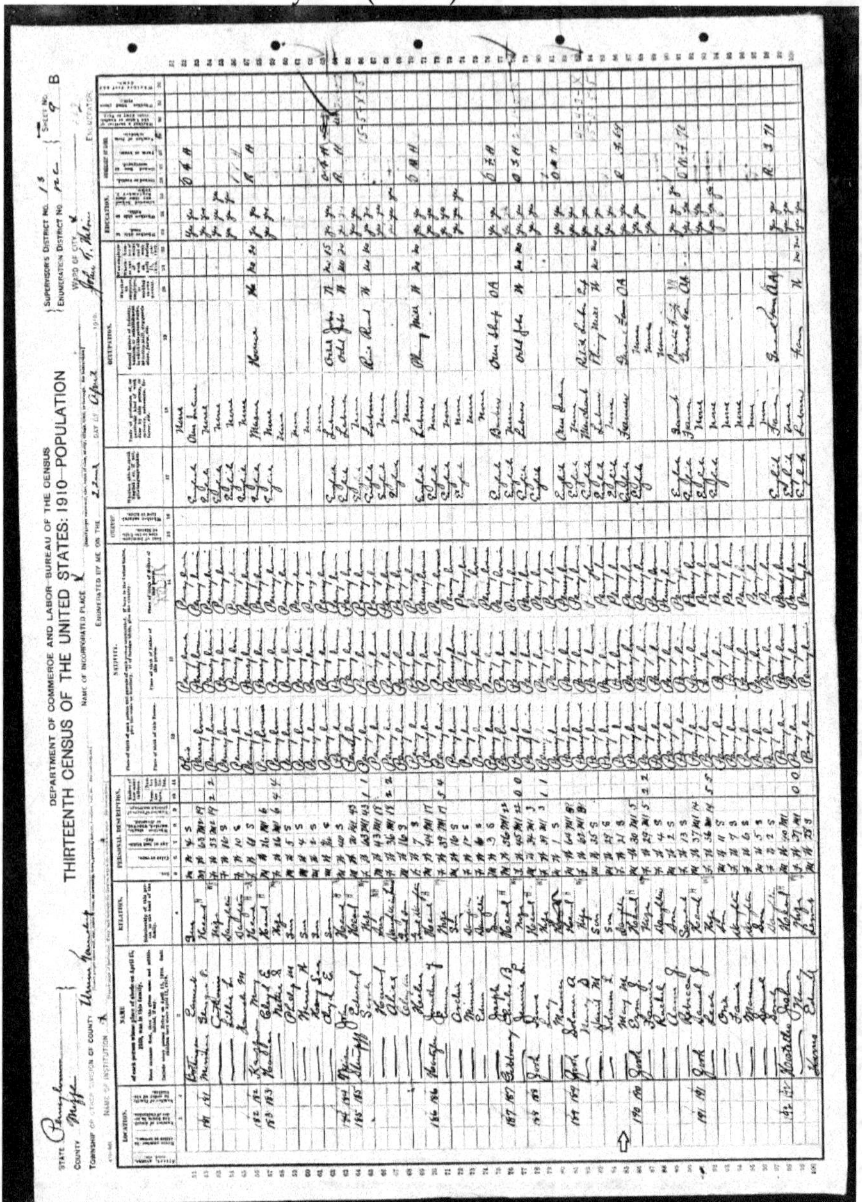

Appendix 4
Obituaries

Obituaries were copied from *Mennobits*, http://www.mcusa-archives.org/mennobits and other newspaper sources.

John H. Yoder (1862)

On the 26th of May, in Spruce Hill Township, Juniata Co., Pa., **JOHN H. YODER,** aged 67 years, 4 months, and 4 days. Funeral sermon was preached by Christian Peachey Mifflin Co. He was sick about 6 months. He leaves a wife and eleven children to mourn their loss.

Fanny (Kauffman) Yoder

YODER.--On the 6th of Jan. 1892, near Spruce Hill, Juniata, Co. Pa., widow **Fanny** Yoder, aged 79 years, 11 months and 9 days. She was the widow of John H. Yoder, who preceded her about 25 years ago. She was a devoted mother of eleven children; of this number seven survive her. She was a daughter of Isaac and Mary **Kauffman**, and a faithful member of the A.M. church. Funeral services by A. Zook and Henry Yoder.

Moses P. Yoder of Belleville, Pa., died Nov. 24, 1910; aged 71 y. 3 m. 10 d. His sufferings lasted about a month from heart trouble and dropsy. During all his illness he was very patient until death relieved him. He was born and raised in Juniata Co., Pa. He is survived by his mother, wife and 3 children. 3 brothers and 4 sisters also survived him. He led a quiet Christian life. Funeral services were conducted from the Locust Grove Amish Mennonite Church, of which he was a faithful member.

> "Call not back the dear departed,
> For his sorrows now are o,er;
> On the borde land we left him,
> Soon to meet, to part no more."

Sarah (Byler) Yoder was born Nov. 21, 1843; died in her home Feb. 19, 1923; aged 79 y. 2 m. 29 d. She was the youngest daughter of Bishop Solomon Byler. She was married to Moses P. Yoder. To this union were born two sons and two daughters. Her husband and daughters preceded her to the spirit world. The two sons, Amos of Orrville, Ohio, and Reuben of Belleville, Pa., survive her. She was of a friendly disposition, meeting every one with a smile. Even in her last sickness she tried to be cheerful when suffering intense pain. Our loss is her eternal gain. She will be greatly missed. In her youth she united with the A. M. Church and remained faithful to the end. The funeral was held at the Belleville Church, conducted by J. D. Yoder and J. H. Byler.

Reuben K. Yoder, Belleville, Pa., son of Moses P. and Sarah **(Byler) Yoder,** was born in Juniata Co., Pa., Oct. 1, 1881; passed away at the Lewistown Hospital, June 11, 1958, following a cerebral hemorrhage; aged 76y. 8 m. 10 d. On July 20, 1911, he was married to Mary M. **Zook,** who survives. Also surviving are 3 sons (Elton, Elmer, and Merle, Belleville, Pa.), 4 daughters (Arvilla-Mrs. Trennis King, Belleville; Pauline-Mrs. Paul King, Troutville; Lola-Mrs. Charles Goss, Lewistown; and Lucille-Mrs. Robert Gotwals, Souderton), one brother (Amos E. Yoder, Orrville, Ohio), 22 grandchildren, and 3 great-grandchildren. An infant daughter and 2 sisters preceded him in death. He was a member of the Maple Grove Church. Funeral services were held at the Trennis King home, June 13, in charge of Raymond Peachey.

Mary M. (Zook) Yoder, daughter of Solomon and Nancy (Kauffman) **Zook,** was born at Allensville, Pa., May 2 1888; died at Mifflintown, Pa., Apr. 5, 1969; aged 80 y. 11 m. 3 d. On July 20, 1911, she was married to Reuben K. Yoder, who died in 1958. Surviving are 7 children (Arvilla - Mrs. Trennis King, Elmer, Elton, Merle, Pauline - Mrs. Paul King, Mrs. Lola Goss, and Lucille - Mrs. Robert Gotwals). She was a member of the

152

Maple Grove Church. Funeral services were held at the Baggus Funeral Home, Belleville, Pa., Apr. 8, with Waldo E. Miller officiating; interment in Locust Grove Cemetery.

Arvilla Mae (Yoder) King
July 19, 2011
Lewistown Sentinel
BELLEVILLE - Arvilla Mae (Yoder) King, 94, of Valley View Haven, Belleville, passed away at 4: 11 p.m. Sunday, July 17, 2011, at the Haven. Arvilla was a devoted wife, mother, mother-in-law, grandmother and great-grandmother.

Born March 10, 1917 in Belleville, she was a daughter of the late Reuben and Mary (Zook) Yoder. She attended Belleville schools and graduated from Belleville High School in 1935. For several years after high school, she was employed as an operator for United Telephone Company.

She married Trennis King at Maple Grove Mennonite Church on April 5, 1942. They purchased the farm east of Belleville from her father where she and Trennis lived for 49 years.

Living along Jacks Mountain, she enjoyed seeing deer, turkeys, and many kinds of birds. In 1996, they moved to a cottage in the Valley View Retirement Community. He preceded her in death in 2002. In 2005, she became a resident of Valley View Haven.

Arvilla is survived by three sons and daughters-in-law, Dennis King and wife Judy, of Lincoln, Neb., Darrel King and wife Sara, of West Liberty, Ohio, and Delmar King and wife Sandy, of Belleville; eight grandchildren and 16 great-grandchildren survive; as well as a sister and brother-in-law, Lucille and Robert Gotwals, of Souderton; and two sisters-in law, Betty Yoder, of Huntingdon, and Ethel Yoder, of McAlisterville.

She was preceded in death by three brothers, Elton, Elmer, and Merle, and two sisters, Pauline King and Lola Goss.

Arvilla was a member of Maple Grove Mennonite Church since childhood.

A funeral service will be held in her honor at 10:30 a.m. Wednesday, July 20, 2011 at Maple Grove Mennonite church with Pastors Galen Sharp, Herb Zook, and Alan Kauffman officiating. Burial will take place at Locust Grove Cemetery. Her family will receive friends from 6 to 8 p.m. Tuesday at Henderson Funeral Home, Belleville.

Should friends desire, memorials may be made to: Maple Grove Mennonite Church, PO Box 955, Belleville, PA 17004 or to Valley View Retirement Community, 4702 East Main St., Belleville, PA 17004.

Arrangements are under the care of Henderson Funeral Home, 3813 West Main St., Belleville, PA 17004.

Arvilla Mae (Yoder) King, 94, Belleville, Pa., died July 17. Spouse: Trennis King (deceased). Parents: Reuben and Mary Zook Yoder. Children: Dennis, Darrel, Delmar; eight grandchildren; 16 great-grandchildren. Funeral: July 20 at Maple Grove Mennonite Church, Belleville.

Trennis S. King, 85, Belleville, Pa., died April 16, 2002. Spouse: Arvilla Yoder King. Parents: Abraham and Katie King (deceased). Other survivors: children Dennis, Darrel, Delmar; eight grandchildren; four great-grandchildren. Funeral: April 19 at Maple Grove Mennonite Church, Belleville.

Pauline Clare (Yoder) King, 85, Goshen, Ind., died March 10, 2006. Spouse: Paul Leonard King (deceased). Parents: Reuben and Mary Zook Yoder. Children: Titus, James, John, Daniel, David, Susanne Berlin; 12 grandchildren; two great-grandchildren. Memorial service: March 18 at College Mennonite Church, Goshen.

Pauline Clare (Yoder) King was born November 5, 1920, in Belleville, Mifflin County, Pennsylvania, the daughter of Mary Mae Zook and Reuben Kauffman Yoder. She died last Friday morning, March 10, 2006, at age 85 after a short illness from the complications of heart irregularities and a stroke.
She lived independently at 1708 South 12th Street, Goshen, Indiana, 46525, until February 27.

Pauline was married to Paul Leonard King on April 1, 1944 in Belleville. He preceded her in death June 3, 1970.

Their children are Susanne Lucille (Richard Berlin), Richmond, Massachusetts; Titus Paul (Joy Kauffman King), Grass Lake, Michigan; Daniel Jacob (Gloria Loucks), Elkhart, Indiana; James Reuben, Lancaster, Pennsylvania; John Robert (Kelli Burkholder), Goshen, Indiana; and David Philip (Patricia Michelsen), Richmond, Virginia. Pauline had 12 grandchildren and 2 great grandchildren.
The family thanks the kind people of Goshen General Hospital, South Bend Memorial Hospital Heart and Cardiac Center, Greencroft Nursing Facility, Elkhart County Hospice, and College Mennonite Church for their able assistance in caring for Mother King and comforting her as she came to a peaceful death.

In lieu of flowers the family encourages donations to Hospital Albert Schweitzer in Haiti. Mother King continued to support medical care there after serving as a volunteer in the 1980s. Haiti is the poorest country in the Western Hemisphere.

The family thanks College Mennonite Church and Yoder-Culp Funeral Home for making arrangements:

> Visitation - in the Koininia Rooms at the church on Friday, March 17, from 2-4 P.M. and again from 6-8 P.M.;
>
> Burial - a family event at Prairie Cemetery on Saturday morning, March 18;
>
> Memorial Service - in the church sanctuary at 11:00 A.M., followed by a meal in the church fellowship room.

Pauline Clare King, 85, of Goshen, Ind., died March 10, 2006, at Greencroft Healthcare. She was born Nov. 5, 1920, to Reuben and Mary (Zook) Yoder in Belleville, Pa.

She married Paul Leonard King on April 1, 1944, in Belleville. She graduated from Lancaster Business College and worked at Big Valley Pennsylvania Bank.

She moved to Goshen in 1959. She was office manager for 17 years for the medical practice of Ernest Smucker and Jon Smucker. She was also a medical secretary for the nursing department of Goshen College and a transcriptionist in the Goshen College Administration Building.

She served two-and-a-half years in the 1980s with Mennonite Central Committee at Hospital Albert Schweitzer in Haiti. She avidly followed current events in Haiti and continued to support medical care in Haiti.

She enjoyed reading and gardening. She was a member of College Mennonite Church of Goshen and a member of Phalo Club.

Survivors include five sons, Titus King and his wife, Joy, of Grass Lake, Mich., James King of Lancaster, Pa., John King and his wife, Kelli, of Goshen, Daniel King and his wife, Gloria, of Elkhart, and David King and his wife, Patricia, of Richmond, Va.; a daughter, Susanne Berlin and her husband, Richard, of Richmond, Mass.; two sisters, Arvilla King of Belleville and Lucille Gotwals of Souderton, Pa.; 12 grandchildren and two great-grandchildren. She was preceded in death by her husband, Paul King, on June 3, 1970; three brothers, Elton, Elmer and Merle Yoder; and a sister, Lola Goss.

Memorial services were held at College Mennonite Church

Paul Leonard King, son of Jacob S. and Ella Mae (Byler) King, was born at Belleville, Pa., Apr. 11, 1920; died unexpectedly at Elkhart, Ind., of a heart attack after passing out awards at an assembly on the last day of school, June 3, 1970; aged 50 y. 1 m. 23 d. On Apr. 1, 1944, he was married to Pauline C. Yoder, who survives. On Sept. 18, 1949, he was ordained minister and served the Rockton and Springville Mission congregations. Surviving are 6 children (Susanne, Titus, Daniel, James, John, and David), one brother (Samuel), and 4 sisters (Effie Mrs. Aaron S. Yoder, Jr., Verna Mrs. Erie Renno, Lydia Mrs. Jos. W. Yoder, and Ruth). He was a member of the College Church, where a memorial service was held June 6 with John Mosemann, Robert Detweiler, and Levi C. Hartzler officiating; interment in the Elkhart Prairie Cemetery.

Lucille (Yoder) Gotwals, 81, of Telford, PA died August 4, 2012 at the same place. She was born October 27, 1930 at Belleville, PA to Reuben and Mary (Zook) Yoder. On July 7, 1951 he/she was married to Robert S. Gotwals, who survives.

Surviving are children, Susan Gotwals (husband Tim Lehman); Brent Gotwals (wife Julie); and Chris Gotwals (wife Kathy), eight grandchildren, and two great-grandchildren.

Memorial services were held August 11, 2012 at Blooming Glen Mennonite Church, Blooming Glen, PA with burial in the adjoining cemetery.

Lucille Y. Gotwals
(October 27, 1930 - August 4, 2012)

Lucille (Yoder) Gotwals - 81, of Telford, PA passed away on Saturday, August 4, 2012 at Lutheran Community at Telford.

She was the loving wife of Robert S. Gotwals for 61 years. Lucy was born in Belleville, PA to the late Reuben & Mary (Zook) Yoder.

She graduated from Belleville High School, class of 1948. Lucy attended Goshen College for 2 years. Lucy became a certified Laboratory Technician through further training at Philadelphia General Hospital. She was employed at Grand View Hospital during the 1950s. Lucy later worked for many years in the family business. She also served as chairwoman of the Goshen College Alumni Board.

Lucy was a member of Blooming Glen Mennonite Church where she served as one of the first women elders for 18 years. She was also a Sunday school teacher, youth sponsor and church administrator. Lucy served in several leadership roles in the Franconia Mennonite Conference.

She was a devoted mother and grandmother who spent many countless hours reading to her grandchildren and playing games with her family. Lucy was an avid tennis player throughout her lifetime. She was a caring and compassionate person, reaching out to many people.

In addition to her husband, she is survived by a daughter, Susan Gotwals & husband, Tim Lehman of Sterling, OH; two sons, Brent Gotwals & wife, Julie of Telford, PA, Chris Gotwals & wife, Kathy of Barto, PA; 7 grandchildren; a step-grand-daughter; 2 step-great-grand daughters, and a sister-in-law, Betty Yoder of Huntingdon, PA.

In addition to her parents, she was preceded in death by three brothers, Elton, Elmer, and Merle Yoder and three sisters, Arvilla King, Pauline King, and Lola Goss.

Visitations will be held on Friday, August 10, 2012 at Blooming Glen Mennonite Church from 6:00 pm - 8:00 pm and on Saturday, August 11, 2012 from 9:00 am - 10:30 am.

A memorial service will be held on Saturday, August 11, 2012 at 11:00 am at Blooming Glen Mennonite Church, 713 Blooming Glen Road, Blooming Glen, Pennsylvania 18911.

Interment will take place in the adjoining church cemetery.

In lieu of flowers, memorial contributions may be made to: Mennonite Central Committee, 21 S. 12th Street Akron, PA 17501.

Arrangements by: Anders-Detweiler Funeral Home & Crematory, 130 East Broad Street, Souderton, Pennsylvania 18964. To send online condolences to the family, visit www.andersfh.com

Lola L. (Yoder) Goss, daughter of Reuben and Mary (Zook) Yoder, was born at Belleville, Pa., July 8, 1925; died of complications from heart surgery at St. Mary's Hospital, Milwaukee, Wis., Apr. 12, 1990; aged 64. On June 23, 1946, she was married to Charles O. Goss, who died m 1965. Surviving are 2 sons (Richard S. and C. Randall), one daughter (Bonnie Watson), 3 sisters (Arvilla King, Pauline King, and Lucille Gotwals), 2 brothers (Elmer and Merle Yoder), and 6 grandchildren. She was preceded in death by one brother. She was a member of Maple Grove Mennonite Church. Funeral services were held at Heller's Burnham Funeral Home on Apr. 16, in charge of Robert L. Hartzler; interment in Mount Rock Cemetery.

Elton Saul Yoder
Son of reuben K. Yoder

The Daily Sentinel

Lewistown, PA

Elton S. Yoder

Elton S. Yoder, 57, formerly of Belleville, died Wednesday, Jan. 19, at 6 a.m. in a Harrisburg hospital.

He was born March 12, 1914, at Belleville, a son of the late Reuben K. and Mary Zook Yoder.

He is survived by two children, Mrs. Gene (Donna) Hensinger of Copperas Cove, Tex., and Ronald Yoder of Thompsontown; and the following brothers and sisters: Elmer of Alexandria, Merle of Huntingdon, Mrs. Trennis (Arvilla) King of Belleville R. D., Mrs. Pauline King of Goshen, Ind., Mrs. Lola Goss of Lewistown, and Mrs. Robert (Lucille) Gotwals of Souderton. Six grandchildren also survive.

Private services will be held at the convenience of the family on Friday in the Baggus Funeral Home at Belleville, with Rev. Donald Plank officiating.

Interment will be made in the Locust Grove Cemetery.

1972

160

Trennis S. King

BELLEVILLE – Trennis S. King, 85, of 501 Oliver Court, Belleville, died at 8:45 p.m. Wednesday, April 16, 2002, at Valley View Haven.

Born April 8, 1917 in Allensville, he was the son of the late Abraham and Katie (Messerman) King. His wife, Arvilla (Yoder) King, whom he married April 5, 1942, survives.

Also surviving are: children, Dr. Dennis and Judy (Harding) King, Lincoln, NE, Darrel and Sara (Yoder) King, West Liberty, OH, Delmar and Sandy (Glick) King, Belleville; a sister, Ethel Yoder, Belleville; eight grandchildren and four great-grandchildren.

He was preceded in death by a sister, Armilda Kauffman.

He graduated from the Allensville Public Schools in 1934.

He farmed near Whitehall and near Woodland before moving in 1947 to the farm east of Belleville where he lived until moving to Valley View Village in 1996. After retiring from farming in 1976, he was a salesman for Agri King and for Hoffman Seeds.

He enjoyed the opportunity to serve his church and community. He was an active member of Maple Grove Mennonite Church where he served as Sunday School teacher for 50 years, and as a member and officer of the Board of Elders and numerous committees. He served on the Belleville Mennonite School Board for many years, 12 years as chairman.

He was one of several men who in the early 1960's initiated what would become the Valley View Retirement Community in Belleville. He served as chairman or vice chairman of the Valley View Board until retiring in 1983. Within the village, King Lane was named to honor his commitment to developing the retirement community.

In 1983, he met with several others interested in the history of the Mennonites in Big Valley. Their meetings resulted in the formation of the Mifflin County Historical Society, which he was chairman of until 1992.

He enjoyed music and over the years, participated in a harmonica quartet as well as in various acapella men's and mixed ensembles and choruses.

A funeral service will be held at 10:30 a.m. Friday at Maple Grove Mennonite Church, Belleville with the Rev. Laban Peachey and the Rev. Gulen Sharp officiating. Interment will follow in Locust Grove Cemetery, Belleville.

Friends may call 6:30 -8:30 p.m. Thursday at Baggus Funeral Home, 3813 W. Main St., Belleville.

Memorial contributions may be made to: Maple Grove Mennonite Church, P.O. Box 995, Belleville, PA, 17004; Valley View Haven, 4702 E. Main St., Belleville, PA 17004; or Belleville Mennonite School, P.O. Box 847, Belleville, PA 17004.

DEATH OF M. P. YODER

Following an illness with dropsy, M. P. Yoder died at his home in Belleville Sunday night at 11 o'clock, aged about 71 years.

Deceased is survived by two sons, A. E. and R. K. Yoder, and one daughter, Mrs. T. E. Zook, all of Belleville. Funeral services will be held at his late home on Wednesday forenoon at 10:30 by Revs. John L. Nast and John Kauffman, followed by interment in the Amish Mennonite cemetery.

Merle Roy Yoder
Retired from Case, New Holland, Belleville

Merle Roy Yoder, 79, of 520 Oneida St., Huntingdon, died at 9:30 a.m. Tuesday, Feb. 14, 2006, at his residence.

Born Oct. 2, 1926, in Belleville, Mifflin County, he was a son of the late Reuben and Mary (Zook) Yoder. He was united in marriage to the former Elizabeth "Betty" Bloss, Aug. 30, 1969, in Hollidaysburg. Mrs. Yoder survives at their home.

Mr. Yoder is also survived by a daughter, Rhonda Letso, Ephrata; and a stepdaughter, Barbara Lea Thomas, Freehold, N.J.; a grandson, Paul Letso Jr., Baltimore, Md.; and a granddaughter, Alissa Jo Letso, New York City, N.Y.

He is also survived by three sisters, Pauline King, Goshen, Ind.; Lucille Gotwall, Souderton; and Arvella King, Belleville.

He was preceded in death by two brothers and a sister, Edwin and Elmer Yoder and Lola Goss.

Mr. Yoder served with the United States Army during World War II and was awarded the American Theatre Service Ribbon and World War II Victory Medal.

He was a member of the VFW Post 5935, Belleville.

Mr. Yoder retired from Case, New Holland in 1989, after a long number of years in the press and shear department.

A resident of Huntingdon County since 1969, Mr. Yoder had resided at his Oneida Street residence since 1971.

A memorial service will be held at 1 p.m. Saturday, Feb. 19, at the Curright-Speck Funeral Home, 207 Ridge Road, Smithfield Township, Huntingdon, with the Rev. Dr. Theodore E. Kiffer officiating. Interment will be made in the Riverview Cemetery.

Memorial contributions may be made to the Home Nursing Agency Hospice, 900 Bryan St., Suite 7, Huntingdon, PA 16652.

Merle R. Yoder

Merle R. Yoder, 79, of 520 Oneida St., Huntingdon, died at 9:30 a.m. Tuesday, Feb. 14, 2006, at home, following an extended illness.

Funeral arrangements, under the direction of the Curright-Speck Funeral Home, 207 Ridge Road, Smithfield Township, Huntingdon, are incomplete at this time. A full obituary will be announced in a later edition of The Daily News.

Elmer D. 'Pop' Yoder

LEWISTOWN — Elmer D. "Pop" Yoder, 78, of Blue Juniata Drive, Lewistown, died at 7:17 a.m. Wednesday, Oct. 27, 1993, at Lewistown Hospital.

Born May 14, 1915, in Belleville, he was a son of the late Ruben and Mary (Zook) Yoder.

Surviving are: children, Mrs. Eugene (Patricia) Bishop, Lewistown RD4, Mary Jane Simpson, Newport News, Va., Mrs. William (Peggy) Knepper, Blue Juniata Drive, Lewistown, Mrs. Vernon (Susan) Daubert, Burnham, Mrs. Gerald (Deborah) Gillette, Camp Hill; brother and sisters, Mrs. Trennis (Arvillia) King, Belleville, Pauline King, Indiana, Luccille Gotwals, Souderton, Merle Yoder, Huntingdon; six grandchildren; nine great-grandchildren.

He was preceded in death by a brother, a sister, a granddaughter and a great-great-granddaughter.

He retired on disability from the Viscose Department of the FMC Corporation in 1957.

He was a member of the F.W. Black Senior Citizens Center, Lewistown.

Services will be held at 10 a.m. Saturday at the Barr Funeral Home, 120 Logan St., Lewistown, with the Rev. Mark Droll officiating. Interment will be in Mooresville Cemetery.

Family will receive friends from 7-9 p.m. Friday at the funeral home.

Memorial contributions may be made to the Lewistown Senior Citizens Center, Buena Vista Circle, Lewistown, Pa. 17044.

Appendix 5

Draft Records
Moses P. Yoder

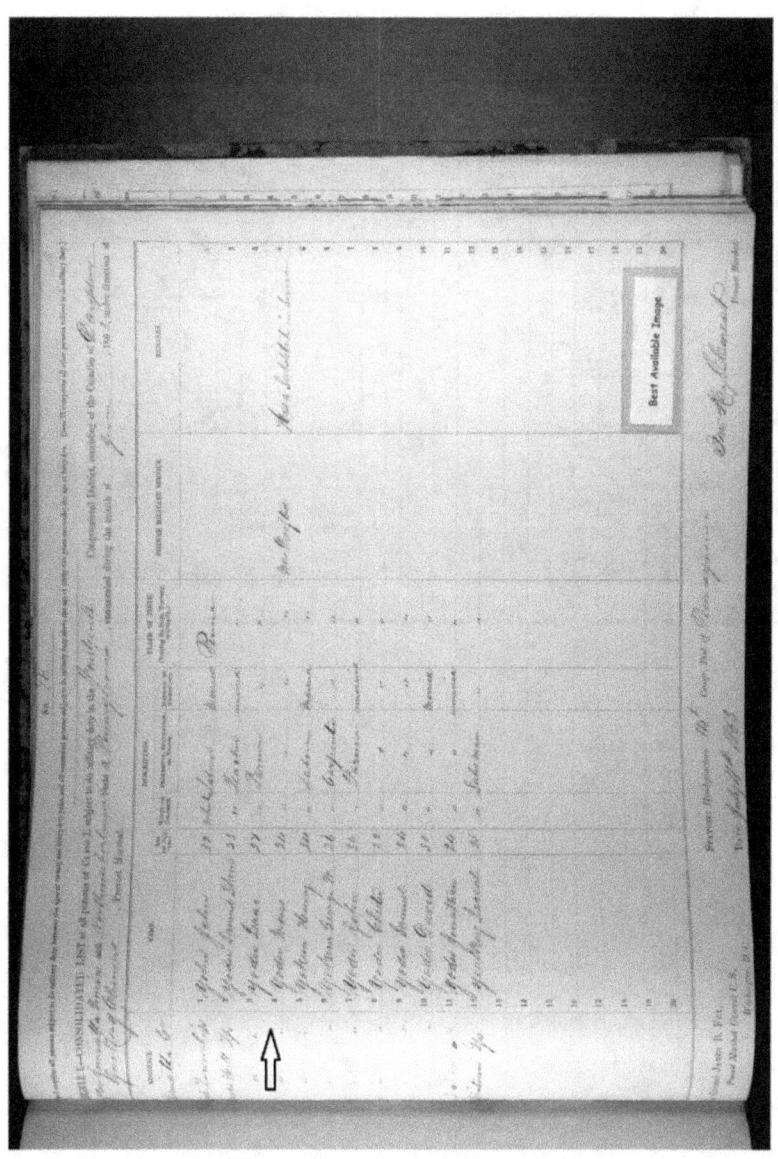

WWI
Draft Records

REGISTRATION CARD—(Men born on or after April 28, 1877 and on or before February 16, 1897)

SERIAL NUMBER 95

1. NAME (Print): Ruben K. (initial only) yoder

ORDER NUMBER

2. PLACE OF RESIDENCE (Print): Walnut St. Belleville, Union Twp, Mifflin Co., Pa.
(Number and street) (Town, township, village, or city) (County) (State)

[THE PLACE OF RESIDENCE GIVEN ON THE LINE ABOVE WILL DETERMINE LOCAL BOARD JURISDICTION; LINE 2 OF REGISTRATION CERTIFICATE WILL BE IDENTICAL]

3. MAILING ADDRESS: Same
(Mailing address if other than place indicated on line 2. If same insert word same)

4. TELEPHONE: Belleville 35-R-11
(Exchange) (Number)

5. AGE IN YEARS: 61
DATE OF BIRTH: 10 - 1 - 1880
(Mo.) (Day) (Yr.)

6. PLACE OF BIRTH: Mifflin Co.
(Town or county)
Penna.
(State or country)

7. NAME AND ADDRESS OF PERSON WHO WILL ALWAYS KNOW YOUR ADDRESS: Mrs. Mary M. Yoder, Walnut St., Belleville, Pa.

8. EMPLOYER'S NAME AND ADDRESS: Self employed

9. PLACE OF EMPLOYMENT OR BUSINESS: Belleville, Mifflin Co., Pa.
(Number and street or R. F. D. number) (Town) (County) (State)

I AFFIRM THAT I HAVE VERIFIED ABOVE ANSWERS AND THAT THEY ARE TRUE.

(Registrant's signature)

D. S. S. FORM 1
(Revised 4-1-42) (over) 16-21680-4

REGISTRAR'S REPORT

DESCRIPTION OF REGISTRANT

HEIGHT (Approx.): 5'7"
WEIGHT (Approx.): 160

EYES: Brown
HAIR: Black
COMPLEXION: Sallow

RACE: White

Other obvious physical characteristics that will aid in identification: None

I certify that my answers are true; that the person registered has read or has had read to him his own answers; that I have witnessed his signature or mark and that all of his answers of which I have knowledge are true, except as follows:

Here to my Knowledge

(Registrar for Local Board)
Carlyle Arnold
3 Lombard, Pa.
(Place of registration)

Date of registration: 4/27/42

Local Board No. 3
Somerset County

APR 27 1942

(STAMP OF LOCAL BOARD)

16-21680-4

Appendix 6

Marriage License
Reuben & Mary Yoder

Appendix 7

Moses P. Yoder
Mifflin County Court Action & Deed
Union Township

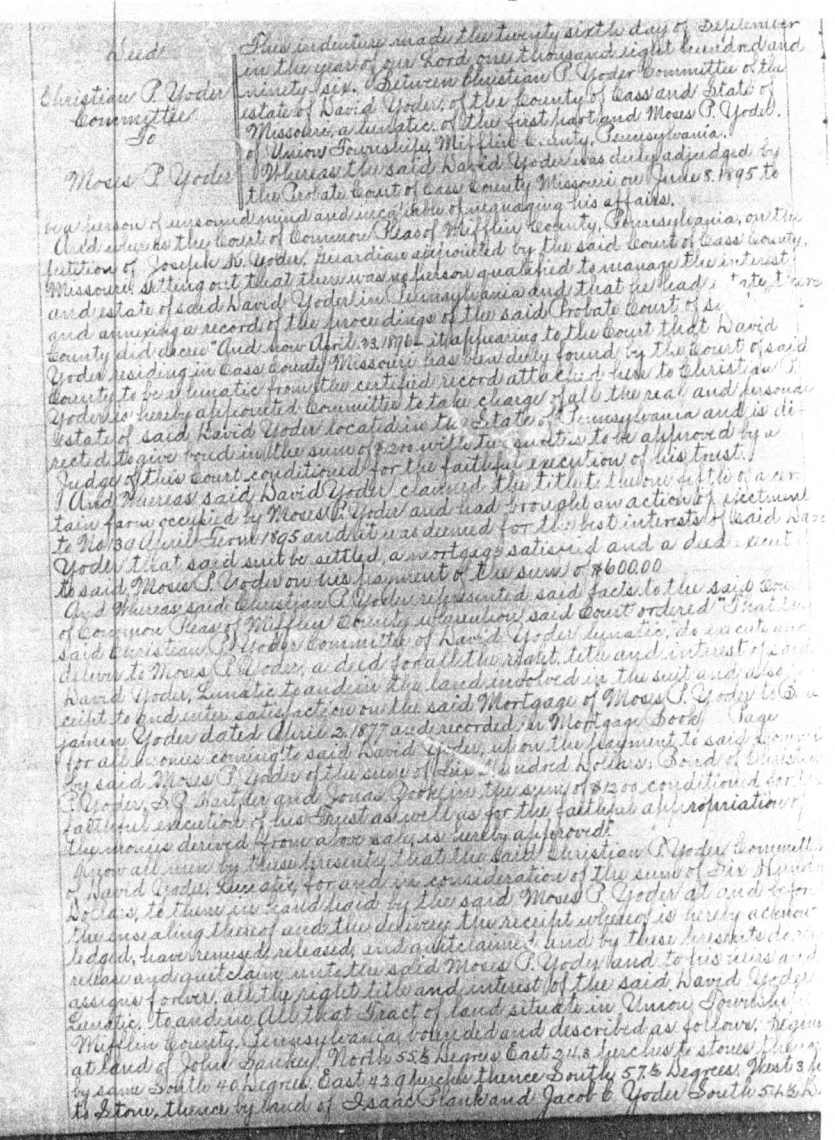

East 215 perches to Stone in Mountain, thence North 50½ Degrees, East 18 Perches to Stone, thence by land of John Peachey, Christian Hostetler and others, North 30½ Degrees, West 208.8 perches to Post thence North 30½ Degrees, West 152.9 perches to Stone thence by land of Sarah King, South 58½ Degrees West 52. 2 perches to Stone, thence North 31 Degrees, West 28.8 perches to Stonelin road, thence by land of George John Yoder South 67½ Degrees West 45.4 perches to stone, thence by land of Jacob E. Yoder South 30½ Degrees, East 145.8 perches to place of beginning containing One Hundred and Forty-two Acres and sixty eight perches and having thereon erected a House, Barn and other improvements. And said Christian P. Yoder Committee of said David Yoder Lunatic does also acknowledge to have received from said Moses P. Yoder satisfaction for all monies owing to said David Yoder on said Mortgage of Moses P. Yoder to Benjamin P. Yoder, dated April 2, 1877 and recorded in the Recorders Office in and for Mifflin County Penna in Mortgage Book "G" page 603 &c and do hereby authorize and empower Samuel L. Coldren, Esq. of Lewistown Penna to enter and enter satisfaction on the record of said Mortgage. And said Christian P. Yoder Committee as aforesaid does also release all claims for mesne profits, arising from said lands or any other claims and demands whatsoever growing out of the possession of the same by the said Moses P. Yoder.

Together with all and singular the hereditaments and appurtenances thereunto belonging or in anywise appertaining and the reversions, remainders, rents, issues and profits thereof and all the estate, right, title, interest, claim or demand whatsoever of him the said David Yoder, either in law or equity of, in and to the above bargained premises. To have and to hold the same to the said Moses P. Yoder and to his heirs and assigns forever. Witness my hand and seal the day and year aforesaid.

Witness present   Christian P. Yoder [Seal]
John M. Wilson   Committee of David
                                                       Yoder Lunatic

Received Sep. 26, 1896 of Moses P Yoder Six hundred Dollars, consideration in full for this Deed.

                                                       Christian P. Yoder
                                                       Committee of David
                                                       Yoder Lunatic

County of Mifflin
State of Pennsylvania, s.s.
        Before me a Justice of the Peace in and for said County and State personally came Christian P. Yoder, Committee of David Yoder, Lunatic, who in due form of law acknowledged the within indenture to be his act and deed and desired that the same might be recorded as such.
In testimony whereof I have hereunto set my hand and seal this 9 day of Oct A. D. 1896.

                                                       John M. Wilson
                                                       Justice of the Peace

                        Ent Nov 7, 1896, @ 10.45 A.M.
                            Recorded & Compared
                                        S. L. Coldren
                                         Recorder

170

Whereas Joseph K. Yoder brought an action of Ejectment against Moses P. Yoder to No. 3 a April Term 1895 of the Court of Common Pleas of Mifflin County, Penna. to recover an undivided one fifth of a certain tract of land in Union Township, Mifflin County, Penna. fully described hereinafter.

And Whereas Joseph K. Yoder as a son and heir of Benjamin P. Yoder was entitled to certain monies secured by a Mortgage of Moses P. Yoder to Benjamin P. Yoder, dated April 2, 1877 and recorded in Mortgage Book "G" page 603 Recorders Office in and for Mifflin County Penna. covering the tract mentioned. And Whereas said Moses P. Yoder has agreed to pay said Joseph the sum of $600.00 in full settlement of said suit, of all right to premises herein and of all matters of difference between them including the of said Joseph K. Yoder in aforesaid mortgage and a conveyance of all of said Joseph K. Yoder in said land.

out the purposes and intents of which settlement the following executed. Know all men by these presents, that the said Joseph K. d Anna Yoder his wife of Cass County Missouri, for and in consid the sum of Six Hundred Dollars, to them in hand paid by the said Yoder at and before the unsealing thereof and the delivery, the receipt hereby acknowledged, have remised, released, and quitclaimed a presents do remise, release and quitclaim, unto the said Moses P d to his heirs and assigns forever, all their right, title and in and in All that Tract of land situate in Union Township County Pennsylvania, bounded and described as follows, Begin and of John Bankey North 55½ Deg. East 24.3 perches to Stones, thence south 10 Deg. East 42.9 perches, thence South 57½ Deg. West 3 per tous, thence by land of Isaac Plank and Jacob C. Yoder South 54½ 215 perches to Stone in Mountain, thence North 50½ Deg. East 18 Stones, thence by land of John Peachey, Christian Hostetler and others, ½ Deg. West 208.50 perches to Post, thence North 30.4 Deg. West 130.50 Stone, thence by land of Sara K. King, South 58½ Deg. West 52.2 stone, thence North 31 Deg. West 28.50 perches to Stones in Road, thence Joseph Byler, South 47½ Deg. West 45.7 perches to Stone, thence by acob A. Yoder South 30½ Deg. East 145.8 perches to place of beginning ng a 148 Acres and 66 perches and having thereon erected a House, Yoder improvements. And they do also acknowledge to have re m Moses P. Yoder all monies owing to said Joseph K. Yoder on afore tgage of Moses P. Yoder to Benjamin P. Yoder, dated April 2, 1877 ded in the Recorders Office in and for Mifflin County Penna in Book "G" page 603 be and do hereby authorize and empower Samuel Esq. of Lewistown, Penna. to appear and enter satisfaction on the record ortgage and do also release all claims for mesne profits arising from of any other claims and demands whatsoever growing out of the poss the same by the said Moses P. Yoder.

with all and singular the hereditaments and appurtenances belonging or in anywise appertaining and the reversions, re rents, issues and profits thereof, and all the estate, right, title, in w or demand whatsoever of us the said Joseph K. Yoder and Anna it herein law or equity of in and to the above bargained premises

To have and to hold the same to the said Moses P Yoder and to his heirs and assigns forever. Witness our hands and seals this first day of August A.D. 1896.

Witness present.   Joseph K. Yoder (Seal)
L.B. Walcomb   Anna Yoder (Seal)

County of Cass
State of Missouri, s.s.

Before me, the subscriber, a Notary Public in and for said County and State, personally came Joseph K Yoder and Anna Yoder his wife who in due form of law acknowledged the foregoing Deed of Release to be their acts and deed and desired that the same might be recorded as such.

And said Anna Yoder being of full age and by me examined separate and apart from her said husband and the contents of the foregoing indenture being first made fully known to her, declared that she did voluntarily and of her own free will and accord, seal sign and as her act and deed deliver the same without any coercion or compulsion of her said husband.

In testimony whereof I have hereunto set my hand and Notarial seal this 31st day of July A.D. 1896.

                                                    Jos S Walcomb
                                                      Notary Public

my comexpires 13th Feb 1898.

Ent. Nov. 7. 1896. @ 11.45 A.M.
Recorded & Compared
                    S. D Coldren
                        Recorder

172

Appendix 8

Christian Yoder YR2
Patent & Land Map

No. 68   CHRISTIAN YODER, YR2
No. 69   CHRISTIAN YODER, YR23

Between them, Christian Yoder, YR2, and his son, Christian
·oder, YR23, warranted four adjacent tracts of land in Penn Town-
·ip and Centre Township. The two southernmost tracts are numbers
? and 14 on the Penn Township Warrantee Map.

Since there is no Centre Township Warrantee Map, the remaining
·o tracts are not found on any warantee map. The data for them is
·ken from the surveys. The data for these four tracts follows:

13
D—9—218
CHRISTIAN YODER
160 Acres and Allowances
Warranted August 28, 1751
Surveyed June 9, 1763
Patented June 19, 1766
To Christian Yoder
AA—8—366
"Contentment"

14
A—33—164
CHRISTIAN YODER
29 Acres and Allowances
Warranted May 9, 1755
Resurveyed October 18, 1805
Patented May 30, 1810

To John Blatt
H—4—113
"Blatt's Palace"

A—33—165
CHRISTIAN YODER
158 Acres and Allowances
Warranted October 27, 1755
Resurveyed October 18, 1805

D—9—214
JOHN HARTLY
Application 1527, dated May 21, 1766
44 1/2 Acres and Allowances
Surveyed August 30, 1766
Returned to Christian Yeodar
November 26, 1766

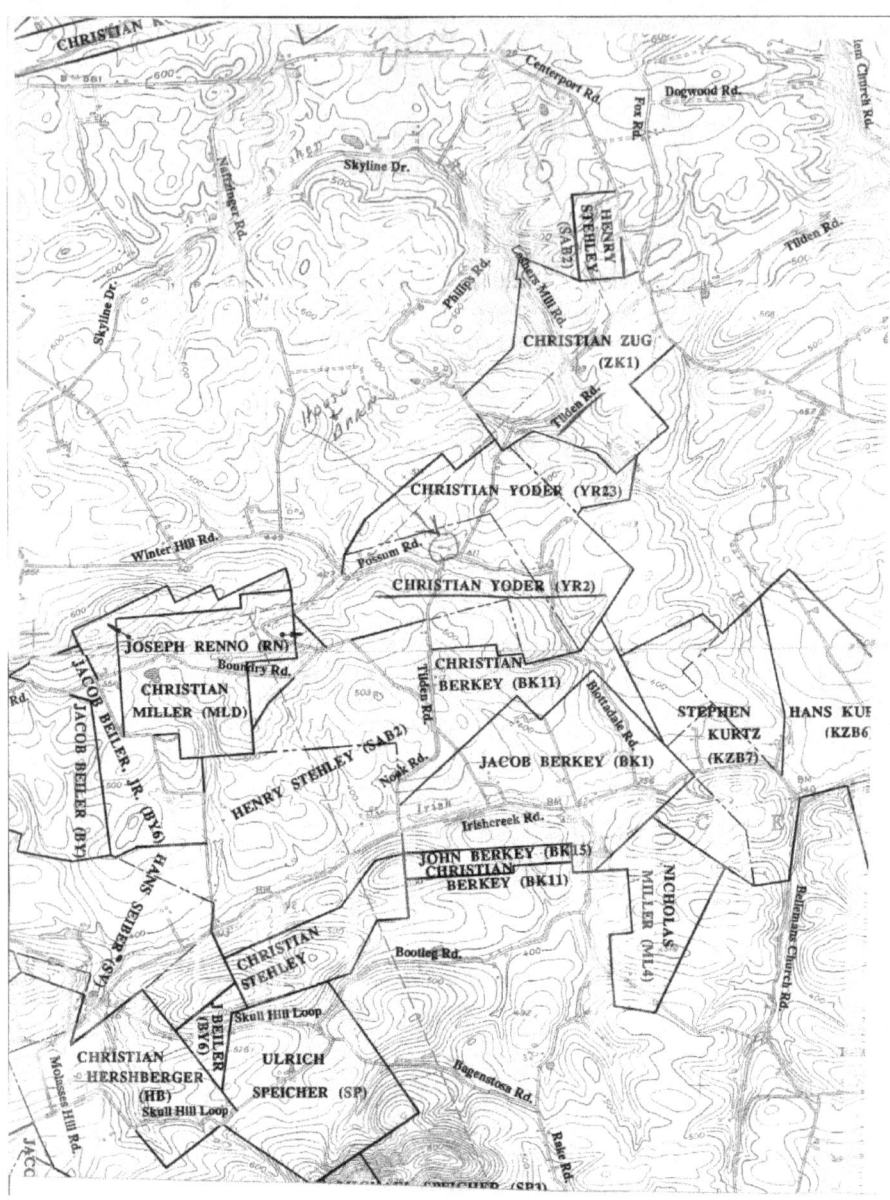

174

Appendix 9

Bishop John Yoder & Henry Milroy
Sales Agreement

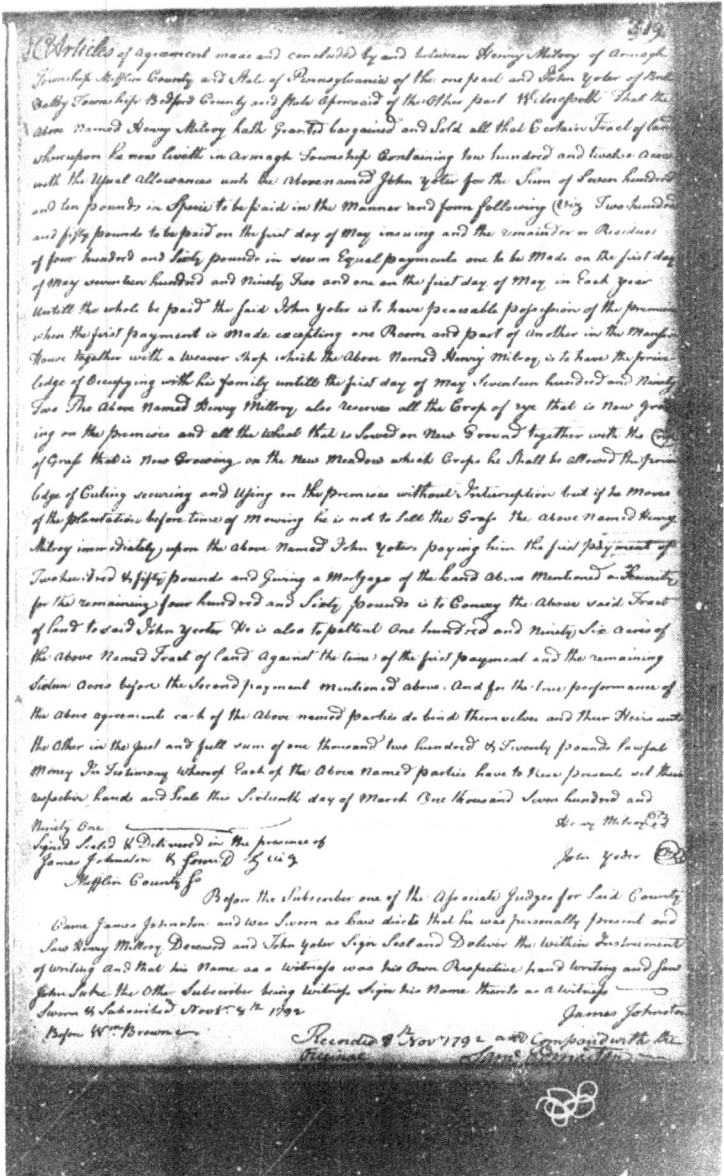

Appendix 10

John H. Yoder YR25111
Will

The last Will of John H. Yoder, of Spruce. Hill. township, Juniata County, Penna.

First. I give to my Wife, Fanny, Four hundred dollars in money or in any of the personal property she may choose to select. And the balance of all my personal effects to be sold. the proceeds thereof to be divided Equally among my Eleven Children.

Second. I direct that all my real Estate To Wit: The Half. Moon farm, Containing one hundred and Sixteen acres, The Hayner tract, adjoining Joshua Hayner, George Rice and James Patterson, Containing ~~Sixty Seven acres but~~ thirteen acres, adjoining Michael Umholtz and The Ridge piece of twenty two acres, adjoining heirs of Shem Hartzler and heirs of Samuel Okeson dec'd, shall be sold four years after my decease, and not sooner. one third of the proceeds thereof (Except the Hayner timber and Ridge pieces) to be and remain Charged on the Half. Moon tract the interest to be paid to my wife Fanny during her life and the principal, at her death, to be divided Equally among all my Children. and the other Two thirds to be divided Equally among all the Children at the time of sale. It is my will, that my Executor hereafter named, sell all said lands, but only under the direction and by order of the Orphan's Court of said County, as in the Case of proceedings in

177

partition with this exception that there is to be no appraisement or valuation prior to the order of sale.

Lastly. I nominate and appoint my son Moses to be the Executor of this my last will. In Witness Whereof I have hereunto set my hand and seal this twenty first day of February A. D. 1867

Signed, Sealed and
declared by the said   John H. Yoder (Seal)
testator as his last
will in our presence
Who witnessed the same
in his presence and at
his request.
Edmund S. Doty
William S Evans

My will now is that the sale of my personal property may be defered for one year after my death provided my Executor my widow and the Guardeens of my Children deem it best and my wish is that the sale of my real Estate may be defered longer that four years provided my Executor my widow and the Guardeens of my minor Children deem it best to do so the time of sale to be fixed by them the above will dated the first day of Feb. A. 1867 to be and remain with this alteration as witness my hand and seal this Signed Sealed and declared by the twenty ninth day of Feb A. 1867 said testator as his last Will
in presence of us who witness the same   John H Yoder (Seal)
in his presence and at his request
J. P. Howell
John Esh

178

Appendix 11

Trivia
Reuben & Mary Yoder Descendants

- We now live in 21 states
- We have 23 surnames
- The furthest migration is to Colorado
- Population by generation:

Generation	8	9	10	11	12
# of Descendants	8	24	44	50	6

- Total number of descendants = 132
- Greatest number of descendants: Elmer 33
- Most Generations: Elmer 5
- Carrying on Yoder family name -
    Elton
        Ronald
            Gregory & Douglas
                Addison, Greer, Graydon,
                Bryce & Zane
- Number of marriages = 70
- 2000 Yoder Census = 44245
- Largest unit prefix "Yotta" = 1 followed by 24 zeros
- Yoder surname rank in 2000 census = 707
- St Joder Day: Aug 17

Descendants

Generation 7	8	9	10	11	12	
	Children	Grandchildren	GG	GGG	GGGG	Total
Reuben & Mary	Alta					1
	Elton	Donna	4	5		20
		Phyllis				
		Ronald	2	5		
	Elmer	Pat	2	5	2	33
		Mary Jane				
		Peggy	1	4	3	
		Susan	3	5	1	
		Deborah Jean	1			
	Arvilla	Dennis	2	3		29
		Darrel	3	8		
		Delmar	3	6		
	Pauline	Susanne	1			22
		Titus	2	1		
		Daniel	2	5		
		John	2	1		
		James				
		David	1			
	Lola	Richard	1	2		12
		Bonita	2			
		Charles	3			
	Merle	Rhonda	2			4
	Lucille	Susan	2			11
		Robert Brent	3			
		Christopher	2			
Total	8	24	44	50	5	132

Descendant Report
Reuben Kauffman Yoder

..... 7 Reuben Kauffman Yoder (1880 - 1958) b: 01 Oct 1880 in Mifflin County, PA, d: 11 Jun 1958 in Lewistown Hospital Lewistown, Mifflin Co, Pa

..... + Mary Mae Zook (1888 - 1969) b: 02 May 1888 in Allensville, Mifflin Co, Pa, m: 20 Jul 1911 in Belleville, Mifflin Co, Pa, d: 05 Apr 1969 in Mifflintown Convalescent Home, Mifflintown, PA

.... 8 Alta Z Yoder (1912 - 1912) b: 18 Jan 1912 in Belleville, Mifflin Co, Pa, d: 20 Jan 1912 in Belleville, Mifflin Co, Pa

.... 8 Elton "Hicks" Saul Yoder (1914 - 1972) b: 12 Mar 1914, d: 19 Jan 1972 in Harrisburg, Pa

.... + Verdie Irene Pearson (1913 - 2009) b: 25 Jul 1913 in Lewistown, Mifflin Co, Pa, m: 11 Aug 1934, d: 22 Jun 2009 in Blairsville, GA Union General Hospital

.... 9 Donna Mae Yoder (1936 -) b: 29 Apr 1936

.... + Gene Wesley Henninger (1938 -) b: 24 Jan 1938, m: 11 Aug 1965 in Saran, Loiret, Centre, France

.... 10 Robert Bryan Henninger (1964 -) b: 30 Jul 1964

.... + Kelly Brown Speckman (1969 -) b: 02 Nov 1969, m: 03 May 1991 in Charlotte, North Carolina

.... 11 Katie "Maelyn" Henninger (1997 -) b: 10 Jan 1997

.... 11 Rachel Brown Henninger (1999 -) b: 19 Sep 1999

.... + Lloyd Colyer

.... 10 Timothy Lloyd Colyer (1952 - 2000) b: 17 Nov 1952, d: 29 Oct 2000 in Waco, TX

.... 10 Donna Diane Colyer (1955 -) b: 02 Nov 1955

.... + Robert Dana Downard (- 2001) d: 2001 in Ft. Worth, TX

.... 11 Alicia Mae Downard (1978 -) b: 29 Nov 1978

.... + Bobbie Jo Talbot m: 14 Jan 1994 in Grapevine, Texas

.... 10 Larry Scott Colyer (1957 -) b: 12 Feb 1957

.... + Patti Gentry (1961 -) b: 15 Aug 1961, m: 15 Sep 1979 in Dillon, Dillon, South Carolina,

.... 11 Megan DeAnne Colyer (1987 -) b: 08 Dec 1987

.... 11 Machaila Kyra Colyer (1998 -) b: 25 May 1998

.... + Pamela Snizer (1957 -) b: 1957 in Waco, TX

.... 9 Phyllis Kay Yoder (1938 - 1943) b: 01 Apr 1938, d: 12 Dec 1943
.... 9 Ronald Fay Yoder (1943 -) b: 02 Apr 1943 in Belleville, PA;
                 Mifflin Co
.... + Gloria Diane Swartzell (1944 -) b: 16 Mar 1944 in
                 Gatesville, TX, m: 24 Mar 1964 in Lewistown, PA; Mifflin
                 Co
.... 10 Gregory Lynn Yoder (1964 -) b: 17 Sep 1964 in
                 Lewistown, Mifflin Co, Pa
.... + Anne Frances Lacerte (1956 -) b: 08 Nov 1956 in
                 Lowell, Ma, m: 25 Oct 1992 in Harvard, Ma
.... 11 Greer Elizabeth Yoder (1995 -) b: 06 Apr 1995
.... 11 Bryce Gregory Yoder (1998 -) b: 02 Dec 1998
.... + Christine Pellman
.... 10 Douglas Wade Yoder (1968 -) b: 29 Feb 1968 in
                 Lewistown, Mifflin Co, Pa
.... + Crystal Lynn Laub (1968 -) b: 19 Mar 1968 in
                 Williamsport, Pa, m: 15 May 1993 in Jersey Shore,
                 Lycoming Co, Pa
.... 11 Addison James Yoder (1994 -) b: 25 Aug 1994 in
                 Ephrata, Pa
.... 11 Graydon Ellis Yoder (1996 -) b: 01 Jan 1996 in
                 Gansvoort, NY
.... 11 Zane Douglas Yoder (1998 -) b: 19 Dec 1998 in
                 Gansvoort, New York
.... 8 Elmer David Yoder (1915 - 1993) b: 14 May 1915, d: 27 Oct 1993
.... + Winifred Belle(Sue) Wilson (1920 - 2007) b: 07 May 1920 in
               Moorestown, Burlington, New Jersey, d: 25 Sep 2007
.... 9 Patricia Louise Yoder
.... + Eugene Samuel Bishop m: 31 Jan 1960
.... 10 Elizabeth Ann Bishop (1962 -) b: 01 Feb 1962 in
                 Lewistown, Mifflin Co, Pa
.... + Steven J. Auker (60 -) b: 29 Mar 60 AD in Lewistown, Mifflin
               Co, Pa, m: 04 Jun 1983
.... 11 Kyle Steven Auker (1986 -) b: 05 Dec 1986
.... 12 Cooper James Auker (2010 -) b: 01 Feb 2010
.... 11 Kayla Elizabeth Auker (1992 - 1992) b: 09 Mar 1992, d:
                 09 Mar 1992
.... 11 Kelsey Elizabeth Auker (1993 -) b: 07 Jun 1993
.... 10 Angela Joy Bishop (1965 -) b: 20 Sep 1965 in Lewistown,
                 Mifflin Co, Pa

.... + Dennis R. Patterson (1963 -) b: 13 Jan 1963, m: 15 Sep 1990

.... 11 Ashlee Sue Patterson (1985 -) b: 15 Oct 1985

.... 12 Cohen Jay Patterson (2007 -) b: 12 Jun 2007

.... 11 Dylan James Patterson (1992 -) b: 09 Jul 1992

.... 9 Mary Jane Yoder (1941 - 2004) b: 22 Oct 1941, d: 28 Apr 2004

.... + Russell Simpson

.... 9 Peggy A. Yoder (1944 -) b: 25 Apr 1944 in Belleville, Mifflin
Co, Pa

.... + William L. Knepper (1936 -) b: 01 Jul 1936 in Burnham, Mifflin
Co; Pa, m: 04 Dec 1960 in New Cumberland, Pa

.... 10 Pamela S. Knepper (1961 -) b: 10 May 1961 in Lewistown,
Mifflin Co, Pa

.... + Raymond Mark Droll (1957 -) b: 01 Apr 1957, m: 30 May
1981 in Lewistown, Mifflin Co, Pa

.... 11 Nathon M. Drall (1982 -) b: 12 Jul 1982 in Mifflin
County, PA

.... 11 Jessica L. Drall (1983 -) b: 16 Aug 1983 in Dermorest,
GA

....   + John Zuch (1984 -) b: 17 Aug 1984, m: 13 Jun
2009 in Toccoa, Stephens, Georgia,

.... 12 Sierra Zuch (2010 -) b: 02 Oct 2010 in Toccoa,
Stephens, Georgia,

.... 12 Roary Zuch (2012 -) b: 08 Mar 2012 in Toccoa,
Stephens, Georgia,

...........................12 Lincoln Michael Zuch b:05 May 2013 Toccoa
Stephans, GA

.... 11 Nicholas W. Drall (1987 -) b: 21 Apr 1987

.... + Anna Long (1990 -) b: 16 May 1990, m: 21 Jul 2012

.... 11 Michael R. Drall (1989 -) b: 30 Aug 1989

.... 9 Susan Lee Yoder (1948 -) b: 25 Jan 1948

.... + Vernon O. Daubert Jr. (1945 -) b: 16 Dec 1945, m: 15 Oct 1966
in Yeagertown Methodist Church, Yeagertown, PA

.... 10 Tracie L. Daubert (1968 -) b: 19 Jan 1968

.... + Jerry Miller (1966 -) b: 19 May 1966, m: 17 May 1996

.... 11 Stephanie S. Miller (1989 -) b: 07 Nov 1989 in
                Lewistown Hospital Lewistown, Mifflin Co,
                Pa
.... + Sam Dye m: 30 Jun 2012
.........................12 Jeffrey Edward Dye b: Sept 2, 2013 Ohio
.... 11 MacKenzie Miller (1998 -) b: 23 Jul 1998 in
                Lewistown Hosp.Lewistown, Mifflin Co, Pa
.... 11 Kylie-Jo E. Miller (2001 -) b: 01 Feb 2001 in
                Lewistown Hosp.Lewistown, Mifflin Co, Pa
.... 10 Joseph V. Daubert (1970 -) b: 19 Oct 1970 in
                Lewistown Hosp.Lewistown, Mifflin Co, Pa
.... + Kathy
.... 11 Amanda M. Daubert (1997 -) b: 30 May 1997 in
                Lewistown Hosp.Lewistown, Mifflin Co, Pa
.... + Laura Lockett m: 22 Feb 2013
.... 11 Adan J. Daubert (2007 -) b: 07 Dec 2007 in
                Lewistown Hosp.Lewistown, Mifflin Co, Pa
.... 10 Brian Lee Daubert (1973 -) b: 24 Jan 1973 in
                Lewistown Hosp.Lewistown, Mifflin Co, Pa
.... 9 Deborah Jean Yoder
.... + Gerald Gillette
.... + Alan Hartley
    .... 10 Michelle Renee Hartley (1971 - 1976) b: Jun 1971, d:
                1976
.... 8 Arvilla Mae Yoder (1917 - 2011) b: 10 Mar 1917 in Belleville,
            Mifflin Co, Pa, d: 17 Jul 2011 in Valley View Haven, Belleville,
            PA Mifflin County
.... + Trennis S. King (1917 - 2002) b: 08 Apr 1917 in Allensville, Mifflin
            Co, Pa, m: 05 Apr 1942 in Belleville, Mifflin Co, Pa, d: 16 Apr 2002
            in Belleville, Mifflin Co, Pa
.... 9 Dennis Samuel King (1947 -) b: 07 Feb 1947 in Reedsville,
            Mifflin Co, Pa
.... + Judy Lynn Harding (1946 -) b: 01 Mar 1946 in
                Montevideo, MN, m: 11 Sep 1970 in Montevideo, MN
.... 10 Katherine Harding King (1979 -) b: 27 May 1979 in
                Lincoln, Lancaster, Nebraska,
.... + Gregory Mitchell (1980 -) b: 28 Feb 1980 in Olathe,
                Johnson, Kansas, m: 01 Jun 2003 in Lincoln, Nebraska,

.... 11 Eleanor Claire Mitchell (2008 -) b: 09 Jan 2008 in
Lincoln, Nebraska,
.... 11 Ian Gregory Mitchell (2011 -) b: 25 Mar 2011 in
Overland Park, Johnson, Kansas,
.... 10 Bradley Dennis King (1976 -) b: 07 Jan 1976 in
Sellersville, Bucks, Pennsylvania,
.... + Jill Fanders (1976 -) b: 28 Apr 1976 in Lincoln,
Lancaster, Nebraska, m: 30 May 1998 in Lincoln,
Nebraska,
.... 11 Isaac Bradley King (2004 -) b: 20 Aug 2004 in
Columbus, Ohio,
.... 9 Darrel Jay King (1948 -) b: 03 Oct 1948 in Belleville, Mifflin
Co, Pa
.... + Sara Jane Yoder (1949 -) b: 02 Dec 1949 in URBANA, OH,
m: 07 Nov 1970 in West Liberty, OH
.... 10 Scott Michael King (1971 -) b: 03 Apr 1971 in
Bellefontaine, OH
.... + Esther Ruth Cole (1984 -) b: 23 Mar 1984 in Cincinnati,
OH, m: 15 Dec 2007
.... 11 Coleson King (2008 -) b: 26 Sep 2008 in Bellefontaine,
OH
.... 11 Truett King (2010 -) b: 19 Feb 2010 in Springfield,
Clark, Ohio,
.... 11 Lachlan King (2011 -) b: 25 Aug 2011 in Springfield,
Clark, Ohio,
.... 10 Anthony J. King (1973 -) b: 16 Jul 1973 in Bellefontaine,
OH
.... + Cynthia M. Madden m: 17 Oct 1992 in Degraff, OH
.... 11 Zachary Garret King (1993 -) b: 02 Apr 1993 in
Bellefontaine, OH
.... 11 Kayla King (1996 -) b: 02 Nov 1996 in Bellefontaine,
OH
.... 11 Hayden King (2003 -) b: 26 Sep 2003 in Bellefontaine,
OH
.... 11 Samantha King (2006 -) b: 02 Oct 2006 in
Bellefontaine, OH
.... 11 Silas King (2006 -) b: 02 Oct 2006 in Bellefontaine, OH

.... 10 Mathew Brent King (1977 -) b: 29 Sep 1977 in
Bellefontaine, OH
.... 9 Delmar Ray King (1952 -) b: 29 Jun 1952 in Belleville, Mifflin
Co, Pa
.... + Sandra Mae Glick (1954 -) b: 09 May 1954 in Lewistown,
Mifflin Co, Pa, m: 30 Jun 1973 in Belleville, Mifflin Co, Pa
.... 10 Crystal Lynn King (1975 -) b: 29 Jun 1975 in Lewistown,
Mifflin Co, Pa
.... + Harold Benfer (1980 -) b: 19 Nov 1980 in Danville,
Montour, Pennsylvania, m: 07 Jul 2007
.... 11 Hunter Lee Benfer (2008 -) b: 10 Sep 2008
.... 11 Chase Benfer (2010 -) b: 02 Nov 2010
.... + Andrew Michael Westover m: Jun 1998
.... 11 Drew Michael Westover (2000 -) b: 24 May 2000
.... 10 Amy Jo King (1977 -) b: 14 Jun 1977 in Lewistown,
Mifflin Co, Pa
.... + Michael A. S. Hood m: 31 May 1996, d: Unknown
.... 11 Megan Nichole King (1996 -) b: 01 Jul 1996
.... + Daniel Robert Aumiller (1974 -) b: 11 Oct 1974, m: 04 Aug
2001
.... 10 Brent Michael King (1980 -) b: 22 Nov 1980 in
Lewistown, Mifflin Co, Pa
.... + Rachel Sellers (1980 -) b: 17 Apr 1980, m: 17 Jul 2004
.... 11 Hanna Marie King (2006 -) b: 17 May 2006
.... 11 Brooke Elizabeth King (2008 -) b: 22 May 2008
.... 8 Pauline Clare Yoder (1920 - 2006) b: 05 Nov 1920 in Belleville,
Mifflin Co, Pa, d: 10 Mar 2006 in Goshen, IN
.... + Paul Leonard King (1920 - 1970) b: 11 Apr 1920 in Belleville,
Mifflin, Pennsylvania, m: 01 Apr 1944, d: 03 Jun 1970 in Elkhart,
Elkhart, Indiana,
.... 9 Susanne Lucille King MD. (1945 -) b: 22 Jan 1945 in Belleville,
Mifflin Co, Pa
.... + Richard Marc Berlin MD. (1950 -) b: 27 Apr 1950 in Jersey
City, NJ, m: 09 Mar 1981
.... 10 Rachel King Berlin MD. (1983 -) b: 20 Feb 1983 in
Columbia, MD
.... + Robert Nelson Gonzalez
.... 9 Titus Paul King (1946 -) b: 30 May 1946 in Belleville, Mifflin
Co, Pa
.... + Joy Amelia Kroft-Kauffman (1942 -) b: 10 Sep 1942 in

186

Eugene, Lane, Oregon, m: 14 Sep 2002

.... + Kathleen Louise Mast (1947 -) b: 20 Mar 1947 in Millersburg, Holmes, Ohio, m: 19 Apr 1969

.... 10 Justin Saul King (1974 -) b: 30 Nov 1974 in Ann Arbor, Washtenaw, Michigan

.... + Sherry Cong Xin Fang (1980 -) b: 08 Feb 1980 in Shanghai, China, m: 23 May 2009

.... 11 Timothy Yi King (2012 -) b: 21 Nov 2012

.... 10 Andre Christian King (1976 -) b: 02 Jul 1976 in Ann Arbor, Washtenaw, Michigan,

.... + Sarah Anne Ries (1976 -) b: 15 Aug 1976 in Brussels (Bruxelles), Belgium, m: 06 Oct 2001

.... 9 Daniel Jacob King (1949 -) b: 17 Jun 1949 in Harrisonburg, Rockingham, Virginia,

.... + Gloria Ann Loucks (1952 -) b: 23 Aug 1952, m: 08 Jul 1972

.... 10 Carmen Sue King (1973 -) b: 22 Sep 1973 in Elkhart, Elkhart, Indiana,

.... + Thomas Shane Snider (1967 -) b: 13 Sep 1967, m: 28 Feb 1998

.... 11 Hayden Thomas Snider (2000 -) b: 18 Jun 2000

.... 11 Hunter Daniel Snider (2003 -) b: 30 Dec 2003

.... 10 Nathan Daniel King (1976 -) b: 12 Apr 1976 in Elkhart, Elkhart, Indiana,

.... + Angela Summer Mishler (1979 -) b: 09 May 1979, m: 17 Mar 2001

.... 11 Brady Nathaniel King (2006 -) b: 15 Apr 2006

.... 11 Austin Daniel King (2007 -) b: 01 Sep 2007

.... 11 Ava Summer King (2010 -) b: 02 Aug 2010

.... 9 John Robert King (1952 -) b: 04 Oct 1952 in Goshen, IN

.... + Kelli (Evelyn) Burkholder (1955 -) b: 28 May 1955

.... 10 Jacob Hans King (1986 -) b: 09 Feb 1986

.... + Carrie Joy Keagy (1984 -) b: 24 Dec 1984, m: May 2010

.... 11 Rivers C. King (2012 -) b: 23 Dec 2012

.... 10 Suzanne Marissa King (1991 -) b: 17 Mar 1991

.... 9 James Reuben King (1952 -) b: 04 Oct 1952 in Goshen, IN

.... 9 David Philip King (1957 -) b: 01 Oct 1957 in DuBois, PA

.... + Unknown m: 09 Jun 1996 in Richmond, VA

.... + Patricia Leonor Michelsen (1952 -) b: 06 Jul 1952 in Bogota, Columbia, m: 09 Jun 1996 in Richmond, VA

.... 10 Alejandro David King (1997 -) b: 17 Jun 1997 in

Richmond, VA

.... 8 Lola Lorraine Yoder (1925 - 1990) b: 08 Jul 1925 in Belleville,
Mifflin Co, Pa, d: 12 Apr 1990 in St. Mary's Hosp, Milwaukee,
Wis

.... + Charles Oscar Goss (- 1965) m: 23 Jun 1946, d: 1965

.... 9 Richard Goss (1947 -) b: 1947

.... + Linda Black (1950 -) b: 1950 in Roaring Spring, PA, m: 1968

.... 10 Mark Goss (1978 -) b: 1978

.... + Jennifer Ludwig (1979 -) b: 1979, m: 2006

.... 11 Reese Goss (2008 -) b: 2008

.... 11 Delaney Goss (2010 -) b: 2010

.... 9 Bonita (Bonnie) Lorraine Goss (1948 -) b: 03 Apr 1948 in
Lewistown, Mifflin Co, Pa

.... + David Haigh Watson (1944 - 2003) b: 03 Dec 1944 in
Lewistown, Mifflin Co, Pa, m: 10 Dec 1971 in Lewistown,
Mifflin Co, Pa, d: 13 Feb 2003 in Lewistown, Mifflin Co,
Pa

.... 10 Angela L. Watson (1972 -) b: 03 Dec 1972 in Lewistown,
Mifflin Co, Pa

.... 10 Kari E. Watson (1980 -) b: 10 Dec 1980 in Lewistown,
Mifflin Co, Pa

.... 9 Charles Randall Goss (1950 -) b: 09 Jan 1950 in Lewistown,
Mifflin Co, Pa

.... + Laura Evelyn Brown (1960 -) b: 17 Jan 1960 in Alexandria,
Va, m: 21 Jul 1984 in Boiling Springs, Pa

.... 10 Nathan Tyler Goss (1986 -) b: 22 Jan 1986 in Harrisburg,
Pa

.... 10 Rebecca Marie Goss (1988 -) b: 09 May 1988 in
Harrisburg, Pa

.... + Donna L. Gearhart m: 1973

.... 10 Michael Alan Goss (1979 -) b: 04 Nov 1979 in Harrisburg,
Pa

.... + Jessica Copenhaver (1981 -) b: 28 Aug 1981, m: 22 May
2010 in Mount Joy, Adams, Pennsylvania,

.... 8 Merle "Mose" Roy Yoder (1926 - 2006) b: 02 Oct 1926 in
            Belleville, Mifflin Co, Pa, d: 14 Feb 2006 in Huntingdon,
            Huntingdon, Pennsylvania,
.... + Arlene Bernice Crownover (1932 -) b: 05 Oct 1932, m: 1948
.... 9 Rhonda M. Yoder (1949 -) b: 21 Feb 1949 in Belleville, Mifflin
            Co, Pa
.... + Paul Letso
.... 10 Paul Letso
.... 10 Alissa Letso
.... + Elizabeth J. Bloss (1924 -) b: 29 Oct 1924, m: 30 Aug 1969
.... 8 Lucille Marian Yoder (1930 - 2012) b: 27 Oct 1930 in Belleville,
            Mifflin Co, Pa, d: 04 Aug 2012
.... + Robert Shueck Gotwals (1929 -) b: 12 Jul 1929 in
            Souderton, PA, m: 07 Jul 1951 in Belleville, Mifflin Co, PA
.... 9 Susan Marie Gotwals (1953 -) b: 20 Jan 1953 in Sellersville,
            Bucks, Pennsylvania,
.... + Timothy Lewman (1952 -) b: 05 Sep 1952 in Berne, IN, m: 11
            Aug 1996
.... + Joseph Anthony Rody (1955 -) b: 17 Aug 1955 in Elkhart,
            IN, m: 24 Jul 1982 in Elkhart, IN
.... 10 Mathew Gotwals Rody (1986 -) b: 13 May 1986 in
            Sellersville, Bucks, Pennsylvania,
.... + Brooke Wyssmann (1980 -) b: 24 Feb 1980 in Mankato,
            MN
.... 10 Sarah Gotwals Rody (1989 -) b: 14 Oct 1989 in Lexington,
            Fayette, Kentucky,
.... 9 Robert Brent Gotwals (1954 -) b: 20 Dec 1954 in Sellersville,
            Bucks, Pennsylvania,
.... + Julia Detweiler (1955 -) b: 19 Sep 1955 in Sellersville, PA, m:
            22 Jul 1978 in Telford, PA
.... 10 Erin Lynn Gotwals (1984 -) b: 22 Nov 1984 in Oregon
            City, Or.
.... 10 Alison Kate Gotwals (1987 -) b: 11 Sep 1987 in
            Sellersville, PA
.... + Andrew Brubaker (1987 -) b: 04 Oct 1987 in Colorado, m:
            31 Jul 2010

.... 10 Jessica Rae Gotwals (1991 -) b: 28 Jan 1991 in Sellersville,
      PA

.... 9 Christopher Kent Gotwals (1965 -) b: 11 Dec 1965 in
      Sellersville, Bucks, Pennsylvania,

.... + Kathleen Schlegel (1962 -) b: 04 Nov 1962 in Reading, Berks,
      Pennsylvania, m: 27 Dec 1996 in Oley, PA

.... 10 Christopher Daniel Gotwals (1999 -) b: 04 Nov 1999

.... 10 Kira Nicole Gotwals (2002 -) b: 19 Aug 2002

Reference
Materials and Organizations

- *Amish and Amish Mennonite Genealogies* by Hugh F. Gingerich and Rachel W. Kreider
- *My Yoder Roots Run Deep* by Ruth F. Yoder Baker
- *The Hertzler-Hartzler Family History* by Silas Hertzler
- *Mifflin County Amish and Mennonite Story* 1791-1991 by S. Duane Kauffman
- *Only A Twig* by Lois Ann Zook
- *The Ol' Hook & Eye* 2nd Edition by John G Hartzler
- *The Yoder Newsletter,* Editor Chris Yoder
- *Mennobits,* http://www.mc-archives.org/mennobits/ A record of Obituaries originated by Don Kauffman and maintained by Mennonite Church
- *Wikipedia,* a free online encyclopedia
- *Mifflin County Mennonite Heritage Center* – Betty Hartzler
- *Juniata County Historical Society*
- *Mifflin County Historical Society*

195

Y

Z

About the Author
Ron Yoder
YR251114423

Ron is the son of Elton S. Yoder and Verdie I. Pearson. He was born on Kisacoquillas St. in Belleville, PA on April 2, 1943.

Ron lived in Belleville until 1952 when, at age 9, his parents separated and he went with his mother to live in Lewistown. Soon after, his father Elton was admitted to a hospital where he remained until his death in 1972.

Ron had no contact with the Yoders until his Aunt Arvilla (Yoder) King contacted him to inform him of his father's death. Arvilla and Trennis very generously offered to make the funeral arrangements.

During the following ten years there was still minimal contact with the Yoders. However, it was in this period that he became interested in his name, his family, who his ancestors were and where he came from.

He grew up hearing about the Amish and how they spoke a form of "German". From this, he assumed that he was of German descent. When he learned that his ancestors were really of Swiss descent, his interest was piqued even more.

Somewhere around 1982 he learned of a man named Chris Yoder who may have additional information. Ron wrote to Chris, providing his lineage back to his grandfather Reuben and asked Chris if he could provide any more information. Chris responded with six more generations. It was also about this time that Ron was introduced to computers. He discovered a "freeware" program to maintain his new found ancestry. This began a love affair of computers and genealogy and was the start of more than thirty years of quest for more and more data and his reintroduction to the Yoders.

Ron is a retired telecommunications executive and, along with his wife Gloria, divides his time between Pennsylvania and Florida. He has two sons and five grandchildren.

www.ingramcontent.com/pod-product-compliance
Lightning Source LLC
Chambersburg PA
CBHW070858290526
45795CB00001B/163